The Debate Book

The Debate Book

EDITED BY
RONALD A. FAUCHEUX

Campaigns & Elections Publishing Company, LLC
Washington, D.C.

Campaigns & Elections Publishing Company., LLC
1555 North 22nd Street, Arlington, VA 22209
202-887-8529

www.debateproject.com
www.faucheux.com

Printed in the United States of America

ISBN 0-9637447-5-5

Library of Congress Control Number: 2003101489
The Debate Book: Standards and Guidelines for Sponsoring Political
Candidate Debates in Congressional, State and Local Elections / [edited
by] Ronald A. Faucheux.-- 1st ed.

Contents

Chapter 5
Nationwide Poll: What Voters Think
About Candidate Debates

Contributors

David Beiler is senior contributing editor of *Campaigns & Elections* magazine and a former member of the Board of Supervisors, Stafford County, Virginia.

Janet Brown is director of the Commission on Presidential Debates.

Diana B. Carlin, Ph.D. is professor of communication studies and dean of the Graduate School and International Programs at the University of Kansas. She was the national coordinator for Debate Watch 1996 and 2000 for the Commission on Presidential Debates.

Michael Cornfield, Ph.D., teaches political strategy and directs research for the Democracy Online Project at George Washington University's Graduate School of Political Management.

Ronald A. Faucheux, Ph.D., editor-in-chief of *Campaigns & Elections* magazine, is a former state legislator in Louisiana and political media consultant. He teaches at the Graduate School of Political Management at George Washington University.

Peter L. Francia, Ph.D., is research fellow at the Center for American Politics and Citizenship at the University of Maryland. He is principal investigator of the Debate Advisory Standards Project

Mark Watts, Ph.D., is a partner of Abacus Associates, a political polling and strategy firm.

INTRODUCTION

Debate Advisory Standards Project

By Ronald A. Faucheux

F ar too little attention has been devoted to political debates below the presidential level. In elections for statewide, district and local offices, debates play a major role in providing information to voters about the candidates.

The Debate Advisory Standards Project, funded through a grant from The Pew Charitable Trusts and sponsored by the Center for American Politics and Citizenship at the University of Maryland, seeks to improve candidate debates by developing nonpartisan standards. The idea is to encourage substantive debates with fair formats and large audiences, and to do so in a comprehensive way that is unrelated to the agenda of any candidate, party or ideology.

For years, there have been no commonly accepted standards or guidelines for political debates that provide practical models for civic, media and political organizations to follow. It is the objective of this book, and other materials and activities of the project, to assist in establishing fair and commonly accepted guidelines for political debates below the presidential level and to encourage their use in federal, state and local elections.

These standards include a series of recommendations and helpful tips based on widespread input to assist in sponsoring and organizing a variety of debate formats and models.

The project has reached out to participants in the political process, the broadcast industry and the civic community to get broad-based input on issues affecting debate sponsorship. Voters across the nation were surveyed to determine citizen attitudes on candidate debate matters. In addition, 611 individual journalists, news directors, editors, civic leaders, debate organizers, media consultants, academics, elected officials and former political candidates were interviewed – in person, by phone and through mail – for this project.

Input has been sought from a wide variety of objective professionals, distinguished academics and public figures as well as political participants representing numerous major and non-major political parties and ideological persuasions.

Based on surveys of political candidates, both winners and losers, it is apparent that there is a need to encourage more opportunities for candidates to engage one another in substantive dialogue about important policy issues.

Candidates themselves, often divided on proposed reforms and changes to the political system, have demonstrated widespread agreement, across party and regional lines, in favor of more public debates. More and better debates, with wider audiences and fair formats, would elevate political campaigning in the United States by providing candidates new, low-cost, issue-oriented channels to communicate their views to the voting public.

Candidate debates are not only important civic and informational exercises, they also can have a substantial impact on candidate standings in competitive elections. During the 2002 elections, for example, debates were thought by many observers to have had a major influence in election outcomes in U.S. Senate races in Missouri, Minnesota, Louisiana and Georgia and in gubernatorial races in Massachusetts and Florida, to name only a few.

Drawing on analysis of existing research and practice, the Debate Advisory Standards Project has identified a series of nonpartisan and nonideological debate guidelines, standards and format models incorporated in this book.

Chapter 1 discusses one of the most difficult issues of debate sponsorship: candidate inclusion. This matter is critical to the candidates and raises substantial questions as to fairness and practicality.

Chapter 2 sets forth standards relative to debate set styles, formats and other matters related to the structure and sponsorship of debates.

Chapter 3 provides a set of model ground rules that can be used in a wide variety of broadcast and non-broadcast debates with different formats and set styles.

Chapter 4 lays out question block options and how they can be consistently structured and applied.

Chapter 5 details results from a nationwide poll of voters on debate issues.

Chapter 6 also discusses voter attitudes on debates, as identified in focus groups sponsored by the project.

Chapter 7 presents ideas on how the Internet can be used to improve debate participation and sponsorship.

Chapter 8 is an interview with Janet Brown, director of the Commission on Presidential Debates. In it, she addresses a range of specific debate sponsorship issues that relate to statewide, district and local elections.

Chapter 9 is a summary of interviews conducted with experienced debate organizers illuminating lessons they've learned.

Chapter 10 is a series of practical "to do" checklists for debate sponsors and participants.

Chapter 11 explains the Debate Watch program and how it can be used to expand citizen participation in political debates.

Chapter 12 is a review of literature and a summary of previous research findings on debates.

CHAPTER 1

Candidate Inclusion

DEBATE ADVISORY STANDARD: For public debates, election campaigns need to be divided into two periods: an *out-period* (more than 30 days before the election) and a *pre-election period* (30 days or less before an election). During the out-period, all candidates with a serious purpose should be invited to debates. During the pre-election period, all candidates with a serious purpose and who have by then demonstrated significant public support should be invited to debates.

There is no more vexing problem in sponsoring political candidate debates than whether to include third-party candidates during general election campaigns and non-major candidates during primary campaigns.

Candidate exclusion is a difficult issue because it requires resolving two legitimate but conflicting principles. The first principle is fairness. Advocates of total inclusion argue that it is unfair to exclude any candidate from participating in a public debate because every candidate has a right to be heard and every voter has a right to hear every candidate.

The second principle is practicality. Advocates of limited inclusion argue that only candidates who have a reasonable chance of winning should participate so that debates afford voters the best opportunity to evaluate only those candidates who are in actual contention. To include minor candidates with little or no chance of winning, they argue, only distracts voters, crowds the debate's format and reduces the amount of time the "major" candidates have to address important issues.

Candidate debate inclusion is not only a matter of principle, it is also a matter of politics. Political analysts have concluded that inclusion of non-major candidates in debates adds credibility to their candidacies and provides them an opportunity to increase their share of the votes on Election Day.

Inclusion of "non-major" and third-party candidates in debates can be a factor even in races where such candidates cannot mount winning campaigns of their own: it can give "minor" candidates the ability to tip the election to one major candidate by siphoning more votes from another.

Establish Two Time Periods

To provide a reasonable balance between the principles of fairness and practicality, it is recommended that there be two time periods in candidate debates: the *out-period* (more than 30 days before Election Day) and the *pre-election period* (30 days or less before Election Day).

It is fair and reasonable that inclusion criteria during the pre-election period may be more difficult to meet than during the out-period. If a non-major or third-party candidate who is given an opportunity to participate in public debates during the out-period does not earn significant public support going into the final 30 days of an election campaign, debate sponsoring organizations that wish to limit participation have an acceptable rationale to tighten the inclusion criteria.

1. *Out-period test.* The test for including a candidate during the out-period should be *seriousness of purpose.* All candidates who have a serious purpose should be included in debates.

Candidates who do not have a serious purpose include "joke" candidates; candidates who do not campaign in a meaningful way; and candidates who admit that their candidacies have only symbolic or trivial intentions.

It is important that non-major and third-party candidates who begin their candidacies with little public support or name recognition are nonetheless equitably provided reasonable opportunities to present their credentials and their positions on the issues during the early stages of an election campaign.

2. *Pre-election period test.* The test for including a candidate during this period should be twofold: *seriousness of purpose* plus *demonstration of significant public support.*

All candidates who demonstrate seriousness of purpose and significant support going into the final 30 days of an election should be included in debates.

▲ Before debate inclusion criteria are determined and before debate invitations are issued, electronic and print media – working together with other debate sponsors such as civic organizations and education institutions – should form a Debate Advisory Standards Board, composed of a representative membership of citizens, to oversee establishing and implementing of candidate inclusion criteria in scheduled debates. It is essential that this process be conducted in a manner that is absolutely fair, nonpartisan and evenhanded.

Criteria for Inclusion: Out-Period

To demonstrate *seriousness of purpose* to be included in debates during the out-period, the candidate shall meet all legal qualifications to hold the office and has either qualified for the ballot or is mounting a write-in campaign for the office sought in accordance with applicable law. In addition, the candidate must meet *one* or more of the following inclusion criteria:

1. The candidate has received 5 percent or more of the vote, tested in a trial heat, in a professionally conducted public opinion survey by an experienced political pollster based on a scientific sample of the entire electorate with a margin of error of less than 5 percent (at a 95 percent level of confidence).

The following may be used as a guide in determining whether a pollster is to be considered "experienced":

(a) The pollster has been a member in good standing of either

the American Association of Political Consultants, the World Association for Public Opinion Research, the American Association for Public Opinion Research or the American Political Science Association for at least three years; or,

(b) The pollster has been employed by news media, educational or other nonpartisan organizations to do national, statewide or congressional district polling with published results; or,

(c) The pollster has been employed professionally by at least three political campaigns or committees to do polling for candidates for statewide, congressional, countywide and/or state legislative offices in at least three elections.

OR

2. The candidate has reported in legal documents filed with federal, state or local governmental entities the receipt, during that election campaign, of at least one campaign contribution per 1,000 residents of the constituency (based on the total number of persons enumerated in the last U.S. census) of $50 or more, excluding contributions received from the candidate himself or herself, the candidate's spouse or the candidate's natural or adopted children. (It should be noted that contributors do not have to be residents of the constituency to be counted.)

OR

3. The candidate previously had been elected to, or held, the office he or she is seeking.

OR

4. The candidate is the official nominee of a political party that: (a) received at least 3 percent of the vote in the most recent gubernatorial general election in the state where the constituency is located; or (b) received at least 3 percent of the vote in the prior presidential general election in the state where the constituency is located; or (c) received at least 5 percent of the vote in the prior general election for the office he or she is seeking.

In states where there are minimum vote requirements for political party ballot access that are generally consistent with the minimums set forth in this section, debate sponsors may choose to substitute the meeting of statutory requirements in place of the provisions in this section.

OR

5. The candidate sought, during the prior eight years, the nomination of a political party in a primary election to the same office he or she is seeking provided, however, that the candidate either (a) won the primary or (b) received a number of votes equal to at least 5 percent of the total number of all registered voters in the constituency in said primary election.

OR

6. The candidate sought the same office during the prior 8 years and received at least 20 percent of the vote in the general election.

OR

7. The candidate met a legal petition requirement to be placed on the ballot, provided, however, that said petition legally required the valid signatures of a number of registered or qualified voters in an amount equal to at least 3 per 1,000 residents of the constituency (based on the total number of persons enumerated in the last U.S. census). In states where there are minimum petition requirements for candidate or political party ballot access that are generally consistent with the minimums set forth in this section, debate sponsors may chose to substitute the meeting of statutory requirements in place of the provisions in this section.

OR

8. (a) *In a statewide, congressional or state legislative election:* The candidate has served, or is currently serving, as governor, as a constitutional officer elected statewide in the state, as a member of the U.S. Senate, as a member of the U.S. House of Representatives, as a member of an elected statewide governing body or as a member of the state legislature in the state where the constituency is located.

(b) In a local, county or municipal election: The candidate has served, or is currently serving, as governor, as a constitutional officer elected statewide, as a member of the U.S. Senate, as a member of the U.S. House of Representatives, as a member of an elected statewide governing body, as a

member of the state legislature, as a countywide elected official, as a member of a countywide governing body, as a citywide elected municipal official or as a member of an elected citywide governing body in the state where the constituency is located.

To illustrate:
• *Charlie Peterson is running for district attorney of Jefferson City, population 223,456. To meet criterion 2, he would need to have raised at least 223 contributions of $50 or more.*

• *John Jones, the Libertarian Party nominee for the state Assembly seat, would meet criterion 4(a) if the Libertarian Party candidate for President of the United States had received at least 3 percent of the statewide vote in the last presidential election.*

• *Mary Smith, the Green Party nominee for mayor of Santa Fe, would meet criterion 4(a) if the Green Party candidate for governor of New Mexico had received at least 3 percent of the statewide vote in the last gubernatorial election.*

• *Bill Thompson, the Natural Law nominee for Congress in the Second District, would meet criterion 4(c) if he had received at least 5 percent of the vote in the Second District in the last general election for Congress.*

• *Jane Martin, who received 16,565 votes in the Democratic primary for Congress in the Third District of her state in the prior congressional election would meet criterion 5 in this election provided that there were 331,300 or fewer eligible or registered voters in the district at the time of her primary election, ensuring that she received at least 5 percent of that total.*

• *Ralph Kelly, a candidate for lieutenant governor, received 21 percent of the vote as an independent candidate for lieutenant governor in the election eight years before. He would meet criterion 6.*

• *Phil Pitts, a Republican candidate for Congress from the Fourth District, had been his party's nominee for Congress from the Fourth District two years before, losing 63–37 percent. He would meet criterion 6.*

• *Sharon Harold is running for governor of a state with a pop-*

ulation of 5,230,775. To get on the ballot, under state law, she needed to collect at least 10,000 valid signatures of registered voters; she actually collected 12,234 valid signatures. If criterion 7 is used, she would not meet it. To meet criterion 7, the legal petition requirement must be at least 15,692 valid signatures ($5,230,775/1,000 = 5,230.775 \times 3 = 15,692$). In this case, even though she submitted more signatures than that amount, it would not qualify because the legal petition requirement (10,000) fell short of that required in criterion 7 (15,692). However, if debate sponsors chose to substitute the state statutory requirement (10,000 signatures) in place of the recommended requirement in this section, then her 12,234 signatures would meet the applicable inclusion criteria.

Criteria for Inclusion: Pre-Election Period

To demonstrate *seriousness of purpose* plus *significant public support* to be included in debates during the pre-election period, the candidate shall meet all legal qualifications to hold the office and has either qualified for the ballot or is mounting a write-in campaign for the office sought in accordance with applicable law. In addition, the candidate must meet *one* or more of the following inclusion criteria:

1. The candidate has received 10 percent or more of the vote, tested in a trial heat, in a professionally conducted public opinion survey by an experienced pollster based on a scientific sample of the entire electorate with a margin of error of less than 5 percent (at a 95 percent level of confidence).

The following may be used as a guide in determining whether a pollster is to be considered "experienced":

(a) The pollster has been a member in good standing of either the American Association of Political Consultants, the World Association for Public Opinion Research, the American Association for Public Opinion Research or the American Political Science Association for at least three years; or

(b) The pollster has been employed by news media, educational or other nonpartisan organizations to do national, statewide or congressional district polling with published results; or

(c) The pollster has been employed professionally by at least three political campaigns or committees to do polling for candidates for statewide, congressional, countywide and/or state legislative offices in at least three elections.

OR

2. The candidate has reported in legal documents filed with federal, state or local governmental entities the receipt, during that election campaign, of at least three campaign contributions per 1,000 residents of the constituency (based on the total number of persons enumerated in the last U.S. census) of $50 or more, excluding contributions received from the candidate himself or herself, the candidate's spouse or the candidate's natural or adopted children.

OR

3. The candidate previously had been elected to, or held, the office he or she is seeking.

OR

4. The candidate is the official nominee of a political party that: (a) received at least 10 percent of the vote in the prior gubernatorial general election in the state where the constituency is located; **or** (b) received at least 10 percent of the vote in the prior presidential general election in the state where the constituency is located; **or** (c) received at least 15 percent of the vote in the prior general election for the office he or she is seeking.

OR

5. The candidate sought, during the prior eight years, the nomination of a political party in a primary election to the same office he or she is seeking, provided, however, that the candidate either (a) won the primary or (b) received a number of votes equal to at least 10 percent of the total number of all registered voters in the constituency in said primary election.

OR

6. The candidate sought the same office during the prior eight years and received at least 30 percent of the vote in the general election.

To illustrate:

• *Tom Dunn, the Libertarian Party nominee for a state Senate seat, would meet criterion 4(b) if the Libertarian Party candidate for president of the United States had received at least 10 percent of the statewide vote in the last presidential election.*

• *George Harvey, the Natural Law Party nominee for mayor of Centerville, would meet criterion 4(a) if the Natural Law Party candidate for governor of her state had received at least 10 percent of the statewide vote in the last gubernatorial election.*

• *Fred Baldwin, the Reform Party nominee for Congress in the Second District of his state, would meet criterion 4(c) if he had received at least 15 percent of the vote in the Second District in the last general election for Congress.*

• *Elizabeth Morris, who received 33,130 votes in the Republican primary for Congress in the Third District of her state in the prior congressional election would meet criterion 5 in this election provided that there were 331,300 or fewer eligible or registered voters in the district at the time of her primary election, ensuring that she received at least 10 percent of that total.*

• *Betty Mario, a candidate for state treasurer, received 22 percent of the vote as an independent candidate for state treasurer in the election eight years before. She would not meet criterion 6.*

• *Doug Snow, a Republican candidate for Congress from the First District, had been his party's nominee for Congress from the First District six years before, losing 68-32 percent. He would meet criterion 6.*

For current election information that may be relevant to the provisions of this chapter, go online for the National Association of Secretaries of State Web site with links to state election offices, at:

http://www.nass.org/sos/sosflags.html

CHAPTER 2

Format Options and Sponsorship Issues

DEBATE ADVISORY STANDARD: Debate formats should be structured to encourage substantive discussion of relevant issues with the voters in mind.

There are five basic political debate set styles:

• *Podium.* This style presents the participants on a stage or in a studio standing behind podiums with fixed microphones. There may or may not be a live audience in attendance.

The podium style is the traditional style used in many televised debates beginning with the first Kennedy-Nixon match-up in 1960. It is relatively simple to stage and to manage, but observers complain that it has a "stiffness" and "formality" that may be off-putting to audiences. Candidates who do not think quickly on their feet and who prefer a more formal setting are usually more comfortable with this format. Having the participants stand at a podium may also raise a host of physical issues, such as the height of the participants and the ability of participants to stand for long periods of time. The format requires strict enforcement of rules.

• *Town Meeting.* This style presents the participants on a stage in front of, or surrounded by, an audience of citizens. Candidates are usually seated on stools and are allowed to walk around the stage.

The town meeting style allows for more audience involvement and accords the participants the most physical flexibility, but it may also be complex to manage. In some cases, with large audiences, it may be difficult to host such an event within the confines of most television studios, which then requires the added expense of an on-location production. It is also difficult to stage such an event when there is a large number of participants on stage. An imbalanced audience may be disruptive and create an unfair advantage for a favored participant. Questioning can be a major issue with this format. Is the audience allowed to ask questions? If so, is there a screening process for question selection? Is there an order to the questioning? Are follow-up questions permitted? Candidates who think quickly on their feet and who excel in informal audience settings are often advantaged with this format.

• *Round Table Conversation.* This style presents the participants on a stage or in a studio seated usually at a round table along with the debate moderator. There usually would not be a live audience in the same room.

The set style tends to encourage conversational discussion – quieter, less formal and emotional – as a result of the more intimate setting, where participants are seated close to one another. This set style works better with less structured rules and puts added demands on the moderator to keep the program in control. It is not recommended without a capable, experienced moderator.

• *Multicandidate Panel.* This style presents the candidates on a stage or in a studio seated at a long rectangular, semicircle or horseshoe-shaped table. The moderator may be seated at a facing table or may be standing at a podium. Additional questioners would be seated at facing tables. There may or may not be an audience in attendance.

The multicandidate panel debate style is often used when there is a large number of participants (four or more). It is a streamlined, efficient approach when there is a large field of candidates either in a primary or a general election. The format may require strict rule enforcement.

• *Interview Show.* Debates are often held as part of pre-existing television or radio talk shows and interview programs. On television, the interview show style usually presents debate participants seated in chairs or on a sofa with the moderator either seated in a chair or seated behind a small desk. In a radio show, the candidates would be seated at tables with microphones, depending upon the number of candidates and the station's production facilities. There usually would not be a live audience in attendance if the debate is broadcast from a TV or radio studio.

There is another variation of the interview show style: the remote interview program. The remote interview show format presents the participants in a studio, seated and looking into cameras. The candidates and the moderator may be in the same studio or in different studios, or even at different locations. The television audience would usually only see a talking-head framed shot of each participant, similar to ABC's *Nightline* program and many other cable and local programs, either full-screen or split-screen. There would not be a live audience in attendance.

Holding debates on existing TV or radio talk shows may encourage more spontaneous discussion. Such programs may rely on the strength and personality of the host and, as a result, may not always encourage a balanced, even handed presentation of participants. This format requires less stringent rules and timekeeping and puts added demands on the moderator to keep the program in control.

Holding debates on existing remote interview TV shows encourages media sponsorship because it can be fit into a 30-minute time block. These shows tend to be highly structured and fast-paced with shorter statements and answers. Because it is essentially an interview program, it may discourage substantive discussion and full treatment of complex issues because it often forces participants to prepackage their statements and answers into short sound bites.

Some recommendations:

▲ In major elections with multiple broadcast debates, the sponsors should work together to ensure that a combination of two or three set styles be used to help offset the advantages and disadvantages of each format as they may apply to the participants.

▲ The interview show has limitations in terms of providing a fair, balanced debate format to encourage the substantive handling of issues by candidates. Consequently, moderators have added responsibility to keep the program moving without discouraging substantive discussion.

▲ Regardless of the debate style, broadcasters should make sure that the set is simple and dignified and that the viewer screen is uncluttered with unnecessary signs and distractions. Sets should not detract from the candidates and what they are saying. Set designs should be subtle, understated and should not intrude into the close-up shots. Staging of broadcast debates should provide the production director the best possible camera shots for the viewing audience.

OPENING AND CLOSING STATEMENTS

DEBATE ADVISORY STANDARD: Candidates in a debate should be allowed an opportunity to make opening and closing statements.

Some observers believe that debates should be question-and-answer programs without giving candidates an opportunity to structure their own statements, especially opening statements. Other observers disagree, and believe candidates should be allowed to make opening and closing statements.

A study of a variety of debates provides ample evidence that even when candidates are not given an opportunity to make opening statements that many of them use some of the time intended for answering their first question to, in effect, deliver an opening statement anyway.

▲ Candidates should be given opportunities to make opening and closing statements in all debate formats.

Here are guidelines for the length of each statement:

Recommended Length of Each Opening or Closing Statement			
Number of Candidates	*Length of Debate Program*		
	90 Minutes	60 Minutes	30 Minutes
2	3 Minutes	2 Minutes	1 Minute
3	2-3 Minutes	1-2 Minutes	45 Seconds
4+	1-2 Minutes	1 Minute	30 Seconds

LENGTH OF DEBATE PROGRAMS

DEBATE ADVISORY STANDARD: Debates should encourage thorough, substantive discussion of relevant topics and issues that goes beyond prepackaged sound bites. In most cases, this requires at least a one-hour debate format.

The length of an overall debate program is a problematic issue for many debate sponsors. In most broadcast debates for major statewide offices – such as U.S. senator and governor – debates are usually 60 or 90 minutes in duration, often depending upon the number of participants. For down-ballot offices, they rarely exceed one hour. Many local television stations attempt to squeeze debates for all offices – statewide, district and local – into pre-existing 30-minute news/talk show formats.

▲ Debate programs should last at least 60-minutes in length.

▲ Debate programs in elections for major statewide offices (U.S. senator and governor) should be 90 minutes in length if (a) they are held during the pre-election period, (b) there are three or more candidates and (c) a combination of question block options is used (see Chapter 4).

▲ When possible, broadcast debate programs in major statewide elections (U.S. senator and governor) as well as other competitive, high-profile elections (U.S. House, big city mayor, etc.) that are scheduled within a 30-minute interview show set style should concentrate on specific issue topics and multiple debates should be held.

LENGTH OF STATEMENTS AND ANSWERS

DEBATE ADVISORY STANDARD: When making statements or answering questions, debate participants should be given adequate time to encourage thorough, substantive discussion of relevant topics and issues that goes beyond prepackaged sound bites.

There are conflicting views on what constitutes the proper length for debate statements and answers. Some argue that lengthier statements and answers encourage more substantive discussion of complex issues and give voters a chance to hear what candidates have to say beyond prepackaged sound bites. Others argue that lengthy answer sequences limit the amount and diversity of questions that can be asked of candidates, as well as follow-up questions, and are generally less interesting to audiences.

The length of opening and closing statements, answers, rebuttals and responses to rebuttals should be a function of the overall length of the debate program and the number of participants. (See page 29.)

PARTICIPANT USE OF PROPS AND VISUALS

DEBATE ADVISORY STANDARD: The focus of political debates should be the participants and their ability to discuss substantive issues. Use of props and visuals should be prohibited.

Though use of props and visuals (charts, posters, books, photographs, etc.) may occasionally assist in explaining substantive issues when properly used, they also pose the risk of distraction, grandstanding and gimmickry. The focus of debates should be the participants and their ability to construct arguments in defense of their positions. Using props and visuals potentially puts too much emphasis on theatrics, especially when they are improperly used.

However, rules relating to props and visuals in most cases are considered too difficult to enforce. Problems involving the number, nature and size of props may confuse and complicate debate preparation.

▲ Candidates should be prohibited from using props and visuals. Debate sponsors should notify all participants in advance of this prohibition.

▲ Debate moderators and questioners should be prohibited from using props and visuals. Debate sponsors should notify moderators and questioners in advance of this prohibition.

PARTICIPANT USE OF NOTES AS PROMPTS

DEBATE ADVISORY STANDARD: Though the focus of political debates should be the participants and their ability to discuss substantive issues, participants should be able to refer to limited notes as prompts.

Unlike props and visuals, debate notes as prompts do not ordinarily pose a substantial risk of distraction from substantive discussions nor do they pose a difficult problem in terms of regulation and enforcement.

▲ Candidates, moderators and questioners should be allowed to bring into the debate notes as prompts to which they can refer throughout the program. Such notes should be placed on the podium, desk or table in front of the speaker. They may be written on letter-sized sheets of paper or index cards that can fit into a letter size business folder or within an ordinary binder up to 2" thick that holds 8-1/2" x 11" pages.

▲ Candidates, moderators and questioners should be allowed to write notes for their own use throughout the program.

▲ In Town Meeting debate programs where the candidates are seated on stools without desks or podiums and may be allowed to walk around the stage, notes as prompts should be limited to allow candidates only to carry on their person or in their hands index-sized cards with notes. Debate sponsors shall notify all participants in advance of this limitation.

NEGOTIATIONS WITH CANDIDATES AND CAMPAIGNS

DEBATE ADVISORY STANDARD: Candidates and campaigns have a right to make sure the rules and format of a debate are fair and evenhandedly applied. However, candidates and campaigns should not be given an opportunity to scuttle or pervert legitimate debate programs.

▲ Candidates and their campaigns may be given, at the discretion of debate sponsors, an evenhanded opportunity to provide reasonable input on *only* the following items:
• The date, time and place of each debate.
• The total number of debates.
• Subject matter.
• The set style of each debate (i.e., town meeting, podium, round table conversation, interview show or multicandidate panel).
• The method of moderator selection.
• The method of questioner selection.
• Type of questioners (i.e., debate moderator, professional journalists, audience members, candidates themselves, academics, civic leaders or other categories of individuals).
• Moderator and questioner names.
• Physical features and format requirements that may impose on any debate participant an unfair disadvantage.
▲ Candidates and campaigns should not be allowed to negotiate or control any other aspect of debate format, rules, enforcement or procedures.

DEBATE SCHEDULING TIME WINDOW

DEBATE ADVISORY STANDARD: Debates should not be held too close to Election Day so that voters have a chance to digest what is said.

▲ No debate should be held within 48 hours of Election Day or on Election Day itself. Debates held in states with early voting, vote-by-mail or liberal absentee voting laws should take this into account when scheduling debates.

▲ In elections for governor, U.S. Senate, U.S. House and mayor of large cities there should be at least one broadcast debate during the out-period before an election and at least two broadcast debates during the pre-election period. In elections for all other offices there should be at least one broadcast debate during the out-period before an election and at least one broadcast debate during the pre-election period.

ISSUING DEBATE INVITATIONS TO CANDIDATES

DEBATE ADVISORY STANDARD: All participants invited to debates should be notified of the time, place and the rules of the program well in advance and they should all be notified at the same time in the same manner.

It is unfair for debate sponsors to invite participants at the last minute. Political candidates are busy people and have intense scheduling pressures. Also, candidates need time to prepare for debates and time to study the rules and format requirements.

▲ Debate invitations should be issued *at least one month* before the scheduled debate. However, in runoffs in which the campaign period is at least four weeks in length but less than eight weeks, or in general elections in which the campaign period after nominees are selected is at least four weeks but less than eight weeks, debate invitations should be issued *at least two weeks* before the scheduled debate; in runoffs in which the campaign period is less than four weeks in length, or in general elections in which the campaign period after nominees are selected is less than four weeks, debate invitations should be issued *at least one week* before the scheduled debate.

▲ Debate participants should be given a complete copy of all rules and format requirements at least five days before the debate (which means all negotiations must cease in time to make this possible).

DEBATE MODERATORS

DEBATE ADVISORY STANDARD: Debate moderators play a crucial role in the sponsorship and management of candidate debates. Moderators must be strictly fair and evenhanded. They also must have adequate experience and training in handling candidate debates as well as a strong knowledge of the substantive issues likely to be raised during a debate. The more experienced and capable a debate moderator, the easier it is to organize debates with a less rigid rule structure.

Selecting experienced, capable, strong, widely respected debate moderators is one of the biggest problems facing media outlets and sponsoring groups in organizing candidate debates. Debate moderators play a crucial role in managing debate programs and in making sure they are conducted fairly and professionally.

Moderators also play a crucial role if one or more of the candidates refuses to abide by the rules. That's why having experience and professional training is so important.

▲ Debate moderators should be provided specific training in: (a) rule enforcement, (b) question-and-answer management and follow-up, (c) technical and equipment requirements, (c) set style development, (d) handling of problem and emergency situations, and (e) the substantive policy issues that may be discussed during the debate.

▲ Professional training programs should be developed and offered to moderators of both broadcast and non-broadcast debates. Professional organizations of broadcasters, news directors and journalists should have input in the preparation of such training programs.

▲ Before each debate, it is suggested that preparation sessions be held without the actual candidates or representatives of the candidates. This mock debate should allow the moderator a warm-up opportunity to practice how to enforce debate rules and how to cut candidates off when necessary.

PROFESSIONAL QUESTIONERS

DEBATE ADVISORY STANDARD: Professional debate questioners must be strictly fair and even-handed. They also must have strong knowledge of the substantive issues likely to be raised during a debate. The opportunity for the audience of average voters to get information they want and need must be the central focus of debate questions.

Professional debate questioners – be they journalists, academics or civic leaders – must ask questions that provide the audience with a fair and balanced view of all the candidates in the debate. The questions should be clear, concise and should be restricted to a single core subject matter.

Questioners must not show bias for or against any point of view, or preference for or opposition to any candidate, in their questioning. They should also not make comments on a candidate's answer if it is not a necessary part of a follow-up question.

▲ A question development process should be put into place by debate sponsors that is based on solid research and diversity of participation.

Briefing files should be prepared on each candidate that include:

(a) biographical information,

(b) news clips,

(c) public statements and issue positions,

(d) legislative voting records,

(e) transcripts of prior interviews and debates, and

(f) content of campaign literature and ads.

These candidate briefing files should be prepared by experienced reporters and/or researchers and held in confidence. They should be shared with the debate moderator and professional questioners.

In preparation for a debate, it is suggested that the individuals who develop the briefing files play a role in question development. This is important to make sure questions are:

(a) relevant in terms of the issues in the election,

(b) penetrating in terms of eliciting information,

(c) substantive in terms of dealing with matters that are important to the elective office being sought,

(d) fair in terms of proper distribution among candidates and subject matters, and

(f) most useful to voters who will watch the debate.

▲ There should be a question practice session before each debate that would include the moderator, the professional questioners and briefing file researchers.

This session would provide an opportunity to assess question relevance and sequence, and may help determine when questions should be followed up. Knowledge of the issues is critical to a questioner's ability to follow up and to the moderator's ability to manage the process. By anticipating candidate answers, and possible evasions, avenues for evasion can be closed off.

"Role playing" is also suggested, when possible. Reporters and researchers who put together the briefing files should develop individual candidate expertise in depth. Then, in discussions of question topics and wording with the moderator and professional questioners, they would be in a position to fully explore questioning opportunities and hazards.

▲ Debate questioners should strive to pose questions that are beneficial to the audience. Questioners should not pose questions that focus on "inside baseball" matters that may be of personal interest to the questioner but of little or no interest to, or usefulness for, the audience.

AUDIENCE QUESTIONERS

DEBATE ADVISORY STANDARD: If questions from the audience are permitted, the process by which questioners are selected must be strictly fair and evenhanded.

▲ When audience members are allowed to ask questions, it is important to:

(a) *Pre-screen questioners* to make sure that the following individuals are not included in the pool of participants who will be allowed to ask questions:

• Staff members and active supporters of any candidate;

• Individuals who have no serious purpose in posing honest and fair questions; and

• Individuals who have exhibited disruptive behavior and lack of respect for debate rules.

(b) *Pre-screen questions* to eliminate:

• Duplication of subject matter;

• Excessive questioner commentary;

• Misstatements of fact or inaccurate claims;

• Biased attacks; and

• Questions that are not clear, concise and direct.

Debate sponsors have the option to either allow audience questioners to directly pose their questions or to submit in writing (usually on index cards) their suggested questions to the moderator who may either read the questions as submitted or restate the wording of the questions when posing them. Debate sponsors may also tape or film questions posed by average voters in "man and woman on the street" interviews conducted by professional journalists.

▲ In general, when there are audience questioners they should be selected on the basis that they do not have a preference for any of the candidates. However, in cases where audience members who have candidate preferences are allowed to ask questions, questioners should be selected in a way that reflects a partisan balance. A questioner who is an active supporter of a candidate, or who holds a position in an organization that has endorsed a candidate, should be so identified when asking a question.

SURROGATES

DEBATE ADVISORY STANDARD: Candidate participation in debates should be strongly encouraged and surrogate participation should be strongly discouraged. In exceptional situations when surrogates are permitted, their participation should be limited.

Political campaigns – especially in statewide elections where proximity to a debate location is an issue – will occasionally send surrogates to debate on behalf of their candidates. Although there are legitimate schedule conflicts and travel burdens that make it difficult (or in some cases impossible) for candidates to participate in debates, having candidates debate surrogates greatly diminishes the importance and usefulness of debates.

In debates where surrogates are used, the dynamic of discussion is altered. In some cases, surrogates are not prepared to adequately handle all of the questions asked and, consequently, do not fully participate in the discussion at hand. In other cases, surrogates simply repeat prepackaged sound bites and campaign slogans without adding to the argumentation process.

When surrogates are, themselves, prominent elected officials, they often speak for themselves and are not always prepared or willing to completely or accurately represent the candidate's views.

In some cases, candidates represented by surrogates are accorded an unfair advantage in that they are given an additional layer of protection against any possible backlash to attacks or missteps.

▲ In broadcast debates and multicandidate forums that are televised or broadcast on radio, taped or live, surrogates should not be allowed. The inability of a candidate to appear in such a debate should be considered, in effect, a nonacceptance of the invitation to debate.

▲ In non-broadcast debates and multicandidate forums held at private or public meetings in which at least one invited candidate is present, surrogates should be permitted to (a) give opening statements, (b) comment on statements or answers provided by candidates who are present and (c) give closing statements.

Questions should only be directed to, or answered by, candidates present. Surrogates should not be allowed to answer questions and should not be allowed to question candidates who are present.

If no candidate is present for a debate, and only surrogates participate, then surrogates should be given the right to answer questions and, where applicable, to ask one another questions.

▲ Surrogates should be allowed to participate in live-audience, non-broadcast, debates if: (a) they appear with the expressed approval of the candidate and (b) the campaign provides notice at least 48 hours before the debate to the event sponsors and to the other invited candidates that a surrogate, by name, will appear to represent the candidate. The only exception to the notice requirement should be an unavoidable, emergency situation.

▲ Candidates should appoint a single surrogate as the campaign's official debate representative and the surrogate should be knowledgeable of the candidate's views and authorized to speak on the candidate's behalf.

▲ In non-candidate ballot issue elections the official campaign committees should appoint debate representatives for all broadcast and live-audience debates. No media outlet in a broadcast debate should allow anyone except an authorized debate representative to appear on behalf of that side of the issue.

RULE ENFORCEMENT

DEBATE ADVISORY STANDARD: When rules are established and participants are given full notice of them, it is expected that all participants will strictly adhere to them without exception.

Enforcement of debate rules can be a difficult matter for a host of reasons:

First, there are few effective sanctions that can be imposed in the case of violations. Second, imposing or failing to impose sanctions may create situations where the appearance of fairness and evenhandedness is jeopardized.

Failure to enforce rules may work to the disadvantage of those participants who are abiding by them and may jeopardize the professionalism and fairness of debate programs.

▲ Debate participants should be required to strictly abide by all rules, provided that the participants were given notice of those rules well in advance of the debate.

▲ Debate moderators should be charged with enforcing rules and doing so fairly and evenhandedly.

▲ When debate rules allow for areas of flexibility and unstructured discussion, the moderator should be charged with making sure the debate discussion is carried out fairly and evenhandedly.

▲ Debate rules should include specific sanctions that the moderator may impose in case of violations:

When a candidate fails to abide by debate rules (i.e., time limits, a prohibition on interrupting other candidates, etc.), the moderator should interrupt the speaker and make the violation known. If the candidate refuses to obey the rules, the moderator should have the option to turn off the speaker's microphone and should issue a warning that repeated violations will result in the candidate being asked to leave the debate. If, after repeated violations, the moderator believes it is necessary for continuation of the debate to require a candidate to leave, the moderator should have that option. If a candidate is required to leave the debate, the moderator shall have the right to allow the candidate to re-enter the debate.

▲ Once rules are established, they shall not be changed or modified unless all candidates are notified of the proposed change or modification before the start of the debate and all candidates assent to it.

CHAPTER 3

Ground Rules

DEBATE ADVISORY STANDARD: All sponsoring organizations should follow a fair, evenhanded and open process when organizing debates. Specific rules and format requirements must be spelled out in advance and provided to all participants in a timely manner.

▲ The following is a model set of ground rules for political debates.

The body of rules presented can be applied to most debates, both broadcast and non-broadcast.

There are additional rules that apply specifically to: (a) broadcast debates, (b) podium debates, (c) multicandidate panel debates, (d) town meeting debates, (e) interview show debates and (f) round table conversation debates.

MODEL DEBATE GROUND RULES

OVERVIEW

Debate Invitations. All candidates who are invited to the debate shall be issued invitations in the same manner and at the same time.

Debate sponsors shall issue invitations to the debate in a fair and evenhanded manner where there is documentary evidence of the time and manner of such invitation.

Debate invitations should be issued *at least one month* before the scheduled debate. However, in runoffs in which the campaign period is at least four weeks in length but less than eight weeks, or in general elections in which the campaign period after nominees are selected is at least four weeks but less than eight weeks, debate invitations should be issued *at least two weeks* before the scheduled debate; in runoffs in which the campaign period is less than four weeks in length, or in general elections in which the campaign period after nominees are selected is less than four weeks, debate invitations should be issued *at least one week* before the scheduled debate.

A debate invitation shall include the exact time and place of the debate and all other relevant information. It also shall include a full explanation of the proposed format and a copy of the proposed ground rules. If one invited candidate's campaign opposes any of the proposals, all invited candidates and their campaigns shall be immediately notified of a negotiation session to settle disagreements related to rules and/or format issues. The exact scope, terms, time and place of such a negotiation session shall be spelled out in the invitation.

Accepting a Debate Invitation. Each invited candidate should be given *at least* a 72-hour period, after receiving the invitation, to decide whether he or she will accept the invitation to debate.

Declining a Debate Invitation. If a candidate does not

accept the invitation to debate, the candidate has a responsibility to notify the debate sponsor in a timely manner and to provide an explanation in writing.

If the invitation was issued at least 30 days before the debate, the notice of declination should be sent within five days of its receipt by the candidate. If the invitation was issued less than 30 days before the debate, the notice of declination should be sent within three days of its receipt by the candidate.

The sponsoring organization shall include the candidate's full statement with reasons for declining the invitation when distributing releases to the news media announcing debate participants.

If a candidate declines a debate invitation, but then changes his or her mind before the debate is held, it is within the discretion of the sponsoring organization to determine whether the candidate should be included.

If multiple candidates have been invited to a debate, and enough candidates accept the invitation to hold the debate, the debate sponsor shall provide candidates who did not accept the invitation to debate an opportunity to submit a short statement of up to 50 words explaining why the invitation was not accepted. If such a statement is submitted by the candidate, and is received by the debate sponsor at least three days before the debate, the debate sponsor shall have the moderator publicly read this statement at the beginning of the debate program.

Communication. Any communication from the sponsoring organization about the debate relevant to the general public, news media or the candidates shall be provided to all the candidates simultaneously.

Negotiations. Debate negotiations shall be held in private and all participants must agree in advance to keep confidential all matters discussed at these sessions.

All invited candidates shall have the opportunity to take part in all negotiating sessions. Each candidate shall designate one negotiator empowered to make final decisions for the campaign.

Early and Equal Access. Each candidate, or appointed representatives of each candidate, shall have supervised access to the debate site and stage area between one and four hours before the debate starts.

Campaign Materials. No campaign materials, literature, hats, stickers, signs or banners are allowed inside the debate hall or studio.

People Accompanying Candidates. When a debate is held in a television studio, the debate sponsor should provide seating, away from the stage, for up to two people who accompany each candidate.

The candidate shall not have access to any person during the debate other than the moderator and the questioners, and, in the case of an emergency, a member of the production crew, sponsor or security staff.

Audience Composition. When there is a live audience beyond a small number of debate sponsors, production crew and campaign staff members, debate sponsors shall ensure that the audience is fairly balanced. In addition to members of sponsoring organizations in attendance, equal numbers of each candidate's known supporters, or known partisans, shall be invited.

If a debate is sponsored by a partisan political organization or advocacy group, and the live audience is to be composed of partisans or issue advocates representing views that may be in conflict with any of the participating candidates, such a situation shall be disclosed in writing to all of the candidates in the invitation to debate as well as in releases to the news media announcing the debate.

Audience Reaction. The live audience will be prohibited from applauding or making noise during the debate and may not do anything visible or audible to express support or opposition to any candidate during the debate.

Candidate Introductions. Candidates will be introduced by the moderator. The introduction shall include: (a) the candidate's name as it will appear on the ballot; (b) the candidate's current public office title (if applicable), former public office title (if not currently a public official) and/or a fair and concise description of his or her current occupation; and (c) the candidate's political party affiliation (if the debate involves candidates of more than one party). Candidates should be introduced in surname alphabetical order.

Candidate Titles. After the introductions, candidates will be referred to as "Mr." and "Ms." Unmarried women may request to be referred to as "Miss" and married women may request to be referred to as "Mrs."

Order of Statements. When there are two candidates participating, the order of opening and closing statements shall be determined by a coin toss before the debate program. The candidate who wins the toss gets to determine whether he or she wants to open first. The candidate who loses the toss gets to determine whether he or she wants to close first.

When there are three or more candidates, the order of opening and closing statements shall be determined by drawing lots (1, 2, 3, etc.) before the debate program. The order for closing statements shall be the reverse of the opening statements, unless all of the candidates agree before the drawing that the order of the closing statements shall be either (a) the same as the opening statements or (b) subject to a second drawing of lots.

Time Limits. Time limits on statements, answers, rebuttals and responses will be strictly enforced.

Timekeeping. The timekeeper shall be someone other than the moderator or a questioner.

In statements or answers that are two minutes or more, there will be three signals given to candidates: the first when there are 30 seconds left; the second when there are 10 seconds left; and the third, a "stop" signal, when the time has run out.

In statements or answers that are *less* than two minutes, there will be two signals given to candidates: the first when there are 10 seconds left; the second, a "stop" signal when the time has run out.

If necessary, the timekeeper shall ring a bell two-to-three seconds after the final "stop" signal is given and the moderator shall immediately interrupt the candidate and discontinue the statement or answer.

Rule Enforcement. The moderator shall enforce all rules and time limits. The moderator may interrupt any participant to enforce the rules and format requirements. The moderator may also take as much time as is needed to explain that a rule has been violated and that the rule was agreed to in advance by all participating candidates.

Disruptive Behavior. If a candidate demonstrates unreasonably disruptive behavior and repeatedly violates the rules, the moderator shall have the right to stop the program, turn off the candidate's microphone and ask the candidate to leave the debate. If a candidate is asked to leave the debate, the remaining candidate or candidates shall be allowed to continue to the end of the program. If a candidate is required to leave the debate, the moderator shall have the right to allow the candidate to re-enter the debate.

If any member of the live audience or any person in the debate facility, invited or not, demonstrates unreasonably disruptive behavior, the moderator shall have the right to stop the program and to ask security to remove the person or persons from the studio or hall.

Adherence to Subject Matter. The moderator may interrupt any candidate if he or she believes the candidate is straying from the subject matter.

Candidate Interruptions. The candidates shall not be allowed to interrupt one another. It is the moderator's responsibility to enforce this rule.

Question Subject Matter. Questions shall relate to one subject only. If a questioner violates this rule, the moderator may restate the question.

Restating Questions. The moderator may restate any question that is unclear.

Question Disclosure. In advance of the debate, debate questioners shall not disclose the substance of any question they intend to ask during the debate to any candidate or representative of any candidate's campaign, or to any person who may communicate the information to a candidate or representative of a candidate's campaign, unless the same information is disclosed at the same time to all of the candidates who are expected to participate in the debate.

The moderator shall disclose to the debate audience when questions were made known to the candidates in advance.

Moderator and Questioner Pre-Debate Statements. Debate moderators and questioners, after their selection, shall make no public statements indicating support or non-support, preference or disrespect, for any candidate expected to participate in the debate.

Closing Statements and Rebuttals. Closing statements made by candidates shall not include charges or attacks against another candidate that have not been previously raised during the debate. If a candidate violates this rule and the attacked candidate has already completed his or her closing statement, the moderator may offer the attacked candidate the right to make a short rebuttal (30 seconds or less), if time permits, after the closing statement segment has been completed.

Accommodating Physical Limitations. The set, format and staging of a debate shall reasonably accommodate the physical limitations of all participating candidates. Candidates have a responsibility to communicate to the debate sponsors any and all considerations they may need due to physical limitations at the time of the debate acceptance.

No Indication of Preference. The set, format and staging of a debate shall in no way show any preference, opposition or disrespect to any of the candidates.

Cameras. Outside of professional photographers or camera crew provided by the debate sponsor, no one in the debate hall shall be allowed to use flash cameras or motor driven cameras during the debate program.

No Distractions. Debate sponsors shall make every effort to avoid anything that may be a distraction to the candidates participating in the debate. That includes adjusting lighting, fixing microphones, opening and closing doors, moving camera equipment and furniture, etc.

Room Temperature. Debate sponsors should ensure that the room temperature is always comfortable for all the participants and within a normal range. To compensate for heat from lighting, room temperature may have to be set lower at the outset of the program.

Media Access. Debate sponsors shall make every effort to accord members of the news media access to the debate program, but to do so in a way that does not disrupt the program or distract the candidates during the program. To accomplish this, an area for the news media should be assigned to allow for arrival and departure photographs of the candidates and post-debate interviews.

Candidate Access. Members of the audience and the news media shall not be given access to candidates when they enter the hall or studio, when they take the stage or at any time in the hour leading up to the debate.

IN ALL BROADCAST DEBATES

Reaction Shots. Televised reaction shots of the candidates will be allowed provided they are balanced and equal in number and length. When reaction shots are aired, the candidate who is speaking should be included in the shot as well as the reacting candidate. (Not to include the candidate who is speaking in the shot may unfairly distract from what he or she is saying at that time.)

No audience reaction shots will be allowed during the debate. Short duration audience pans during the debate are allowed only during a break or when the moderator or a questioner is speaking.

Before the debate, the policy on reaction shots must be explained to all candidates.

Commercial Breaks. Commercial breaks during debates are discouraged. However, when commercial breaks are required, they should be kept to a minimum and timed to fall at logical times to coincide, when possible, with a change in questioners or question blocks. Broadcasters should not sell or place any political, party, issue or advocacy advertisements during debate commercial breaks.

Split Screens. When there is a split screen with two or more candidates on camera at the same time, the size of each candidate's share of the total screen area shall be equal to that of the other candidate or candidates on camera at the same time.

IN PODIUM DEBATES

Candidate Positions. Each candidate is to remain behind his or her podium for the entire debate. Stools will be provided for each candidate.

Water. A glass or bottle of water will be provided on each podium.

Props and Visuals. Candidates may not bring or use props or visuals (charts, posters, signs, banners, etc.).

The moderator and questioners may not bring or use props or visuals (charts, posters, signs, banners, etc.).

If a candidate violates this rule, the cameras will not focus on, and to the extent possible will not show, the props or visuals.

Notes. Candidates are allowed to bring into the debate notes they can use as prompts and may refer to them throughout the program. Such handwritten or typed notes should be placed on the podium in front of the candidate. They may be written on letter-size sheets of paper or index cards that can fit into a letter-size business folder or within an ordinary binder up to 2" thick that holds 8-1/2" x 11" pages. Candidates shall refrain from holding up to camera view as signs or props any of their notes, papers, binders or folders.

Candidate materials. Each candidate shall be given a note pad and two working pens with black ink. Candidates also are allowed to bring their own writing instrument and may write notes for their own use throughout the debate program.

IN MULTICANDIDATE PANEL DEBATES

Candidate Positions. Each candidate is to remain behind his or her table where seated.

Water. A glass or bottle of water will be provided on the table or nearby.

Notes. Candidates are allowed to bring into the debate notes they can use as prompts and may refer to them throughout the program. Such handwritten or typed notes should be placed on the table in front of the candidate. They may be written on letter-size sheets of paper or index cards that can fit into a letter-size business folder or within an ordinary binder up to 2" thick that holds 8-1/2" x 11" pages. Candidates shall refrain from holding up to camera view as signs or props any of their notes, papers, binders or folders.

Candidate materials. Each candidate shall be given a note pad and two working pens with black ink. Candidates also are allowed to bring their own writing instrument and may write notes for their own use throughout the debate program.

IN TOWN MEETING DEBATES

Candidate Positions. Stools will be provided for each candidate. Candidates are permitted to walk within a designated area on stage while speaking.

Water. A glass or bottle of water will be provided to each candidate on a small table next to his or her stool.

Props and Visuals. Candidates may not bring or use props or visuals (charts, posters, signs, banners, etc.).
The moderator and questioners may not bring or use props or visuals (charts, posters, signs, banners, etc.).

Notes. Candidates are allowed to bring into the debate notes they can use as prompts and may refer to them throughout the program. Such handwritten or typed notes should be kept on the candidate's person, held in the candidate's hand or neatly placed on the table with the glass or bottle of water. Notes are not to be used as props or visuals.

IN ROUND TABLE CONVERSATION DEBATES

Candidate Positions. Candidates are to be seated in alphabetical order by surname. Candidates are not allowed to stand up or to walk around during the debate program.

Water. A glass or bottle of water will be provided on a small table next to each candidate.

Props and Visuals. Candidates may not bring or use props or visuals (which includes charts, posters, signs, banners, etc.).

The moderator and questioners may not bring or use props or visuals (which includes charts, posters, signs, banners, etc.).

Notes. Candidates are allowed to bring into the debate notes they can use as prompts and may refer to them throughout the program. Such handwritten or typed notes may be kept on the candidate's person or placed neatly on the table in front of the candidate. They may be written on letter-size sheets of paper or index cards that can fit into a letter-size business folder or within an ordinary binder up to 2" thick that holds 8-1/2" x 11" pages. Candidates shall refrain from holding up to camera view as signs or props any of their notes, papers, binders or folders.

Candidate Materials. Candidates also are allowed to bring their own writing instrument and may write notes for their own use throughout the debate program.

IN INTERVIEW SHOW DEBATES

Candidate Positions. Chairs will be provided for each candidate. Candidates are not permitted to get out of their chairs.

Water. A glass or bottle of water will be provided to each candidate on a small table next to his or her chair.

Props and Visuals. Candidates may not bring or use props or visuals (charts, posters, signs, banners, etc.).

The moderator and questioners may not bring or use props or visuals (charts, posters, signs, banners, etc.).

Notes. Candidates are not allowed to bring into the debate prepared notes and may not make notes throughout the debate program.

CHAPTER 4

Question Block Options

DEBATE ADVISORY STANDARD: The structure and rules of the question-and-answer process of a debate must be clearly spelled out in advance for the benefit of all participants. The sequence, order and length of time given to each candidate for answers and statements should be designed to encourage substantive handling of the issues and must be as consistent, fair and evenhanded as possible.

The building block of a candidate debate is the question block. Question blocks include asking the question, the initial answer, any follow-up question and answer (when allowed), and any rebuttals and response to rebuttals (when allowed). There are many types of question blocks that can be used.

You can have single-candidate question blocks in which the question is asked of only one candidate. You can have all-candidate question blocks in which the same question is asked of all participating candidates. You can have candidate cross-questions in which one candidate asks another candidate a question. In all three types, you may allow the opposition to rebut the answers and you also may allow the candidate who answered the initial question to respond to the opposition rebuttals.

Some question blocks can be highly structured, where statements are set in sequence to make sure that every candidate can comment the same number of times in an established order. Other question blocks can be unstructured, where the rules are few and the moderator is given wide latitude to manage the discussion to make sure every candidate is treated fairly.

The question blocks you select are usually a function of the (a) length of the debate, (b) number of participating candidates, (c) number of questioners, (d) type of questioners and the (e) format and (f) nature of the debate. A 90-minute podium debate with two candidates will necessarily be different from a 30-minute interview show debate with three candidates or a 60-minute multicandidate panel debate with six candidates.

In structuring a debate, you must first add up (a) the amount of time it will take for the moderator to welcome the audience and to introduce the participants (usually 1 to 2 minutes), (b) the amount of time it will take for each candidate to give an opening statement (if opening statements are allowed), (c) the amount of time for each candidate to give a closing statement (if closing statements are allowed) and (d) the amount of time it will take for the moderator to sign off (usually less than 30 seconds).

In a 90-minute debate with two candidates, 3-minute opening statements and 3-minute closing statements, you will have about 78 minutes available for question blocks.

The following pages outline question block formats and are presented according to the number of candidates in a debate (two to six). The more candidates participating, the more complicated question blocks become when they involve all candidates and when they allow rebuttals and responses to the rebuttals.

Generally, questioners should be given up to 30 seconds to pose questions.

The length of answers will necessarily vary depending on (a) the length of the debate program and (b) the number of candidates in the debate. For purposes of these standards, we recommend debate sponsors use one of the following three sequence lengths:

• A *short* answer sequence would include up to a 1-minute initial answer, a 30-second rebuttal and a 30-second response to the rebuttal. Answers to follow-up questions also would be limited to 30 seconds. Follow-up questions may be asked only by the moderator.

• A *regular* answer sequence would include up to a 2-minute initial answer, a 1-minute rebuttal and a 30-second response to the rebuttal. Follow-up answers also would be limited to 1 minute.

• A *long* answer sequence would include up to a 3-minute initial answer, a 90-second rebuttal and a 45-second response to the rebuttal. Follow-up answers also would be limited to 90 seconds.

Answer sequences must be consistent within a question block. For example, a 3-minute initial answer should not be followed by a 30-second rebuttal.

The following answer sequence lengths are recommended (based on the number of candidates participating in the debate and the length of debate program):

Answer Sequence Length

Recommended for 30/45-Minute Debate Program:

2 Candidates	Regular or Short Answer Sequence
3 Candidates	Short Answer Sequence
4 Candidates	This program length not recommended for 4 candidates
5+ Candidates	This program length not recommended for 5+ candidates

Recommended for 60-Minute Debate Program:

2 Candidates	Regular or Long Answer Sequence
3 Candidates	Regular Answer Sequence
4 Candidates	Regular or Short Answer Sequence
5+ Candidates	Short Answer Sequence

Recommended for 90-Minute Debate Program:

2 Candidates	Regular or Long Answer Sequence
3 Candidates	Regular or Long Answer Sequence
4 Candidates	Regular Answer Sequence
5+ Candidates	Regular or Short Answer Sequence

It should be noted that 30- and 45-minute debate programs are not recommended when there are four or more candidates participating.

▲ The following question blocks are recommended for both broadcast and non-broadcast debates (three recommended answer sequence length options are in parentheses):

Question Block A:
Single-Candidate Question Block With No Rebuttal

 • *Questioner (or Moderator) asks Candidate A a question* (up to 30 seconds)
 • *Candidate A answers* (1 minute/2 minutes/3 minutes)

COMMENT: Question block "A" is the simplest. It includes a question directed to only one candidate and an answer, without follow-up or rebuttal. The shortcoming of this question block is that it does not allow for candidate rebuttal, which is an essential element in most debate formats. This block would more often be used in multiple candidate debates with a short program length.

Question Block B:
Single-Candidate Question Block With Rebuttal

In a two-candidate debate:
  • *Questioner (or Moderator) asks Candidate A a question* (up to 30 seconds)
  • *Candidate A answers* (1 minute/2 minutes/3 minutes)
  • *Moderator gives Candidate B the opportunity to rebut*
  • *Candidate B rebuts* (30 seconds/1 minute/90 seconds)

COMMENT: The "B" block includes a question directed to only one candidate, an answer and a rebuttal opportunity. It should be noted that this question block option should only be used when there are two candidates. A 30-second response to the rebuttals should be accorded to Candidate A when there are three or more candidates participating in the debate. This protects Candidate A from being "ganged up on" by multiple opponents without having a chance for a final word in response.

Question Block C:
Single-Candidate Question Block With
Rebuttal and Response

In a two-candidate debate:

• *Questioner (or Moderator) asks Candidate A a question* (up to 30 seconds)
• *Candidate A answers* (1 minute/2 minutes/3 minutes)
• *Moderator gives Candidate B the opportunity to rebut*
• *Candidate B rebuts* (30 seconds/1 minute/90 seconds)
• *Moderator gives Candidate A the opportunity to respond*
• *Candidate A responds* (30 seconds/30 seconds/45 seconds)

In a three-candidate debate:

• *Questioner (or Moderator) asks Candidate A a question*
• *Candidate A answers* (1 minute/2 minutes/3 minutes)
• *Moderator gives the other candidates an opportunity to rebut*
• *Candidate B rebuts* (30 seconds/1 minute/90 seconds)
• *Candidate C rebuts* (30 seconds/1 minute/90 seconds)
• *Candidate A responds* (30 seconds/30 seconds/45 seconds)

COMMENT: The "C" block includes a question directed to only one candidate, an answer and rebuttal opportunity for the opposition. It can be used with any number of candidates. The above illustrates two- and three-candidate debates. The initial question can be asked by the moderator or another questioner.

In a two-candidate debate, question block "C" can use up to 2 minutes and 30 seconds with the short answer sequence, 4 minutes with the regular answer sequence and 5 minutes and 45 seconds with the long answer sequence.

In debates with more than two candidates, you would add up to 30 seconds/1 minute/90 seconds, respectively, for each additional candidate's rebuttal.

Question Block D:
Single-Candidate Question Block With
Structured Follow-Up, Rebuttal, Response

In a two–candidate debate:

• *Questioner (or Moderator) asks Candidate A a question* (up to 30 seconds)
• *Candidate A answers* (1 minute/2 minutes/3 minutes)
• *Questioner (or Moderator) follows up with a question (if needed)* (up to 30 seconds)
• *Candidate A answers* (30 seconds/1 minute/90 seconds)
• *Moderator offers Candidate B the opportunity to rebut*
• *Candidate B rebuts* (30 seconds/1 minute/90 seconds)
• *Moderator offers Candidate A a chance to respond*
• *Candidate A responds* (30 seconds/30 seconds/45 seconds)

In a three–candidate debate:

• *Questioner (or Moderator) asks Candidate A a question* (up to 30 seconds)
• *Candidate A answers* (1 minute/2 minutes/3 minutes)
• *Questioner (or Moderator) follows up with a question (if needed)* (up to 30 seconds)
• *Candidate A answers* (30 seconds/1 minute/90 seconds)
• *Moderator offers the other candidates an opportunity to rebut*
• *Candidate B rebuts* (30 seconds/1 minute/90 seconds)
• *Candidate C rebuts* (30 seconds/1 minute/90 seconds)
• *Moderator offers Candidate A an opportunity to respond*
• *Candidate A responds* (30 seconds/30 seconds/45 seconds)

COMMENT: The "D" block includes a single-candidate question, an initial answer, a structured opportunity for the questioner to follow up (or the moderator, if the initial question was not asked by the moderator), a follow-up answer, opposition rebuttal and a response to the rebuttal.

In a two-candidate debate, question block "D" can use up to 3 minutes and 30 seconds with the short answer sequence,

5 minutes and 30 seconds with the regular answer sequence and 7 minutes and 45 seconds with the long answer sequence.

In debates with more than two candidates, you would add up to 30 seconds/1 minute/90 seconds, respectively, for each additional candidate's rebuttal.

This question block is best used in the podium and multicandidate panel debate styles.

Question Block E:
Single-Candidate Question Block With Rebuttal and Unstructured Follow-Up Discussion

In a two-candidate debate:

• *Questioner (or Moderator) asks Candidate A a question (up to 30 seconds)*
• *Candidate A answers* (1 minute/2 minutes/3 minutes)
• *Questioner (or Moderator) may follow up with Candidate A and/or Candidate B and is to moderate an unstructured discussion (including rebuttals and responses) between both candidates provided that each statement made by a candidate is limited (30 seconds/1 minute/90 seconds, depending upon the answer length sequence used). The amount of time allocated to this unstructured discussion period is determined by the moderator but generally should not exceed an overall period of time (3 minutes/4 minutes/5 minutes, depending upon the answer length sequence).*

In a three-candidate debate:

• *Questioner (or Moderator) asks Candidate A a question (up to 30 seconds)*
• *Candidate A answers* (1 minute/2 minutes/3 minutes)
• *Questioner (or Moderator) may follow up with Candidate A and is to moderate an unstructured discussion (including rebuttals and responses) between all the candidates provided that each statement made by a candidate is limited (30 seconds/1 minute/90 seconds, depending upon the answer length sequence used). The amount of time allocated to this unstructured discussion period is determined by the moderator but generally should not exceed an overall period of time (3 minutes 30 seconds/4 minutes 30 seconds/5 minutes 30 seconds, depending upon the answer length sequence).*

COMMENT: In debate block "E," a time limit needs to

be placed on the unstructured discussion period. This time limit should be placed generally at 3 minutes when using the short answer question sequence, 4 minutes when using the regular answer question sequence and 5 minutes when using the long answer question sequence.

In a two-candidate debate, question block "E" generally uses up to 4 minutes 30 seconds with the short answer sequence, 6 minutes and 30 seconds with the regular answer sequence and 8 minutes 30 seconds with the long answer sequence.

In debates with more than two candidates, you would add time for each additional candidate.

This question block is well-suited to the round table conversation style debate and is not recommended for debates with more than four candidates.

Question Block F:
Lightning Round All-Candidate Question Block

In a two-candidate debate:

• *Questioner (or Moderator) asks Candidates A and B the same question* (up to 30 seconds)
Moderator directs Candidate A to answer
• *Candidate A answers* (up to 30 seconds)
• *Moderator directs Candidate B to answer*
• *Candidate B answers* (up to 30 seconds)

In a three-candidate debate:

• *Questioner (or Moderator) asks all the candidates the same question* (up to 30 seconds)
Moderator directs Candidate A to answer
• *Candidate A answers* (up to 30 seconds)
• *Moderator directs Candidate B to answer*
• *Candidate B answers* (up to 30 seconds)
• *Moderator directs Candidate C to answer*
• *Candidate C answers* (up to 30 seconds)

COMMENT: In an all-candidate "lightning round" a question is asked of all the candidates, who then have an opportunity to provide a short answer (usually 30 seconds or less). In some debates, one-word ("yes" or "no") answers are required.

When requiring especially short answers, it is essential that the questions are asked in a fair way so candidates are not automatically boxed out of providing needed explanations.

Lightning round question blocks are most appropriate at the end of a debate when there is not enough time remaining for longer blocks. Often, the moderator will determine, based on available time, how long the candidates' answers will be.

In a two-candidate debate, question block "F" can use up to 1 minute and 30 seconds.

In debates with more than two candidates, you would add the time allocated for each additional candidate's rebuttal.

This question block is best used in podium and multican-didate panel debates.

Question Block G:
All-Candidate Question Block Without Rebuttals

In a two-candidate debate:

• *Questioner (or Moderator) asks Candidates A and B the same question* (30 seconds)
• *Moderator directs Candidate A to answer*
• *Candidate A answers* (1 minute/2 minutes/3 minutes)
• *Moderator directs Candidate B to answer*
• *Candidate B answers* (1 minute/2 minutes/3 minutes)

In a three-candidate debate:

• *Questioner (or Moderator) asks Candidates A and B the same question* (30 seconds)
• *Moderator directs Candidate A to answer*
• *Candidate A answers* (1 minute/2 minutes/3 minutes)
• *Moderator directs Candidate B to answer*
• *Candidate B answers* (1 minute/2 minutes/3 minutes)
• *Moderator directs Candidate C to answer*
• *Candidate C answers* (1 minute/2 minutes/3 minutes)

COMMENT: The "G" block is a question directed to all candidates in which there is no opportunity for opposition rebuttal.

In a two-candidate debate, question block "G" can use up to 2 minutes and 30 seconds with the short answer sequence, 4 minutes and 30 seconds with the regular answer sequence and 6 minutes and 30 seconds with the long answer sequence.

In debates with more than two candidates, you would add up to 1 minute/2 minutes/3 minutes (depending upon the answer length sequence) for each additional candidate's answer.

A question block without rebuttals limits the value of candidate debate discussion by not allowing candidates to comment on one another's answers.

Question Block H:
All-Candidate Question Block With Rebuttals

In a two-candidate debate:

• *Questioner (or Moderator) asks Candidates A and B the same question* (30 seconds)
• *Moderator directs Candidate A to answer*
• *Candidate A answers* (1 minute/2 minutes/3 minutes)
• *Moderator directs Candidate B to answer*
• *Candidate B answers* (1 minute/2 minutes/3 minutes)
• *Moderator offers Candidate A a chance to rebut*
• *Candidate A rebuts* (30 seconds/1 minute/90 seconds)
• *Moderator offers Candidate B a chance to rebut*
• *Candidate B rebuts* (30 seconds/1 minute/90 seconds)

In a three-candidate debate:

• *Questioner (or Moderator) asks Candidates A and B the same question* (30 seconds)
• *Moderator directs Candidate A to answer*
• *Candidate A answers* (1 minute/2 minutes/3 minutes)
• *Moderator directs Candidate B to answer*
• *Candidate B answers* (1 minute/2 minutes/3 minutes)
• *Moderator directs Candidate C to answer*
• *Candidate C answers* (1 minute/2 minutes/3 minutes)
• *Moderator offers Candidate A a chance to rebut*
• *Candidate A rebuts* (30 seconds/1 minute/90 seconds)
• *Moderator offers Candidate B a chance to rebut*
• *Candidate B rebuts* (30 seconds/1 minute/90 seconds)
• *Moderator offers Candidate C a chance to rebut*
• *Candidate C rebuts* (30 seconds/1 minute/90 seconds)

COMMENT: The "H" block is a question directed to all candidates in which there is an opportunity for opposition rebuttal.

In a two-candidate debate, question block "H" can use up to 3 minutes and 30 seconds with the short answer sequence,

6 minutes and 30 seconds with the regular answer sequence and 9 minutes and 30 seconds with the long answer sequence.

In debates with more than two candidates, you would add up to 1 minute 30 seconds/3 minutes/4 minutes 30 seconds (depending upon the answer length sequence) for each additional candidate's answer and rebuttal.

This question block is best used in the podium, town meeting and multicandidate panel styles.

Question Block I:
All-Candidate Question Block With Structured Follow-Ups and Optional Rebuttals

In a two-candidate debate:

• *Questioner (or Moderator) asks Candidates A and B the same question* (up to 30 seconds)
• *Candidate A answers* (1 minute/2 minutes/3 minutes)
• *Questioner (or Moderator) may follow up with Candidate A* (up to 30 seconds)
• *Candidate A answers* (30 seconds/1 minute/90 seconds)
• *Moderator directs Candidate B to answer*
• *Candidate B answers* (1 minute/2 minutes/3 minutes)
• *Questioner (or Moderator) may follow up with Candidate B* (10-30 seconds)
• *Candidate B answers* (30 seconds/1 minute/90 seconds)
• *Moderator has the option to offer both Candidate A and Candidate B a chance to rebut*
• *Candidate A may rebut* (30 seconds/1 minute/90 seconds)
• *Candidate B may rebut* (30 seconds/1 minute/90 seconds)

In a three-candidate debate:

• *Questioner (or Moderator) asks all candidates the same question* (up to 30 seconds)
• *Candidate A answers* (1 minute/2 minutes/3 minutes)
• *Questioner (or Moderator) may follow up with Candidate A* (up to 30 seconds)
• *Candidate A answers* (30 seconds/1 minute/90 seconds)
• *Moderator directs Candidate B to answer*
• *Candidate B answers* (1 minute/2 minutes/3 minutes)
• *Questioner (or Moderator) may follow up with Candidate B* (10-30 seconds)
• *Candidate B answers* (30 seconds/1 minute/90 seconds)
• *Moderator directs Candidate C to answer*
• *Candidate C answers* (1 minute/2 minutes/3 minutes)
• *Questioner (or Moderator) may follow up with Candidate C*

(10–30 seconds)
- *Candidate C answers* (30 seconds/1 minute/90 seconds)
- *Moderator has the option to offer all candidates a chance to rebut*
- *Candidate A may rebut* (30 seconds/1 minute/90 seconds)
- *Candidate B may rebut* (30 seconds/1 minute/90 seconds)
- *Candidate C may rebut* (30 seconds/1 minute/90 seconds)

COMMENT: The "I" block is an all-candidate question in which the questioner may follow up on each question and there is an opportunity for opposition rebuttal. This is one of the longest question blocks because of the time it may take to pose and answer follow-up questions.

In a two-candidate debate, question block "I" can use up to 5 minutes and 30 seconds with the short answer sequence, 9 minutes with the regular answer sequence and 13 minutes and 30 seconds with the long answer sequence.

In debates with more than two candidates, you would add up to 2 minutes/4 minutes/6 minutes (depending upon the answer length sequence) for each additional candidate's answer and rebuttal. Obviously, this question block becomes too long to use in most debate programs with a large number of candidates.

This question block is best used in podium and multi-candidate panel debate styles.

Question Block J:
All-Candidate Question Block With
Unstructured Follow-Up Discussion

In a two–candidate debate:

• *Questioner (or Moderator) asks Candidate A and Candidate B the same question (up to 30 seconds)*
• *Candidate A answers* (1 minute/2 minutes/3 minutes)
• *Candidate B answers* (1 minute/2 minutes/3 minutes)
• *Questioner (or Moderator) may follow up with Candidate A and/or Candidate B and is to moderate an unstructured discussion (including rebuttals and responses) between the candidates provided that each statement made by a candidate is limited (30 seconds/1 minute/90 seconds, depending upon the answer length sequence used). The amount of time allocated to this unstructured discussion period is determined by the moderator but generally should not exceed an overall period of time (3 minutes/4 minutes/5 minutes, depending upon the answer length sequence).*

In a three–candidate debate:

• *Questioner (or Moderator) asks the candidates the same question (up to 30 seconds)*
• *Candidate A answers* (1 minute/2 minutes/3 minutes)
• *Candidate B answers* (1 minute/2 minutes/3 minutes)
• *Candidate C answers* (1 minute/2 minutes/3 minutes)
• *Questioner (or Moderator) may follow up with any of the candidates and is to moderate an unstructured discussion (including rebuttals and responses) between the candidates provided that each statement made by a candidate is limited (30 seconds/1 minute/90 seconds, depending upon the answer length sequence used). The amount of time allocated to this unstructured discussion period is determined by the moderator but generally should not exceed an overall period of time (3 minutes 30 seconds/4 minutes 30 seconds/5 minutes 30 seconds, depending upon the answer length sequence).*

COMMENT: The "J" block is an all-candidate question and answer that allows for an unstructured follow-up discussion that can extend for a period of time at the discretion of the moderator.

In a two-candidate debate, question block "J" can generally use up to 5 minutes and 30 seconds with the short answer sequence, 8 minutes and 30 seconds with the regular answer sequence and 11 minutes and 30 seconds with the long answer sequence.

In debates with more than two candidates, generally add up to 1 minute 30 seconds/2 minutes 30 seconds/3 minutes 30 seconds, depending upon the answer sequence length.

This question block is best used in the round table conversation style debate, and is not recommended for debates with more than three candidates.

Question Block K:
2-Candidate Cross-Question Block With
Rebuttal and Response

- *Moderator directs Candidate A to ask Candidate B a question*
- *Candidate A asks Candidate B a question* (up to 30 seconds)
- *Candidate B answers* (1 minute/2 minutes/3 minutes)
- *Moderator offers Candidate A an opportunity to rebut*
- *Candidate A rebuts* (30 seconds/1 minute/90 seconds)
- *Moderator offers Candidate B an opportunity to respond*
- *Candidate B responds* (30 seconds/30 seconds/45 seconds)

In a three-candidate debate, you have the option of either (a) restricting candidate cross-questions to only two candidates (as in a two-candidate debate) or (b) allowing the third candidate (who neither asks the question nor answers initially) an opportunity to rebut the initial answer. Where the third candidate is allowed to join in to rebut the answer, the question block would follow accordingly:

- *Moderator directs Candidate A to ask Candidate B a question*
- *Candidate A asks Candidate B a question* (up to 30 seconds)
- *Candidate B answers* (1 minute/2 minutes/3 minutes)
- *Moderator offers Candidate A an opportunity to rebut*
- *Candidate A rebuts* (30 seconds/1 minute/90 seconds)
- *Moderator offers Candidate C an opportunity to rebut*
- *Candidate C rebuts* (30 seconds/1 minute/90 seconds)
- *Moderator offers Candidate B an opportunity to respond*
- *Candidate B responds* (30 seconds/30 seconds/45 seconds)

COMMENT: The "K" block provides for one candidate to ask another candidate a question with an opportunity for a rebuttal and response.

In a two-candidate debate, question block "K" can use up to 2 minutes and 30 seconds with the short answer sequence, 4 minutes with the regular answer sequence and 5 minutes and 45 seconds with the long answer sequence.

In a debate with three or more candidates, when the third,

fourth, fifth, etc., candidate is allowed to rebut, you would add up to 30 seconds/1 minute/90 seconds, depending upon the answer sequence length, for each candidate.

Question Block Lead-Ins:

I. Audience Member Direct Question

• *Moderator introduces the citizen questioner*
• *Questioner asks the question (up to 30 seconds) of either a single candidate or of all candidates (depending upon rules)*
• *Moderator clarifies question, if necessary; directs candidate(s) to answer*

This lead-in is used in a town meeting style debate when audience members are allowed to ask direct questions.

II. When Audience Member Questions Are Restated

• *Moderator introduces the audience member who has submitted the question. The moderator then asks that question and restates it, if necessary, for clarity* (up to 30 seconds)

This lead-in is used in a town meeting style when audience members are allowed to submit questions and the moderator actually poses the question. The moderator may restate the question to ensure clarity and that the question has a single core subject matter.

III. Combination Studio/On-Location Question Introduction

• *Moderator (in studio) introduces the questioner (on location)*
• *Questioner introduces an issue (up to 30 seconds)*
• *Questioner tosses to a tape clip of a citizen or citizens discussing the issue/problem (up to 1 minute)*
• *Questioner asks the question (up to 30 seconds)*
• *Moderator directs candidate(s) to answer*

This format variation calls for the studio moderator to introduce a questioner (usually a professional journalist) to introduce an issue/problem. The questioner then tosses to a tape clip of a voter or voters discussing the issue/problem in a way that does not indicate candidate preference or partisan bias. After the tape clip, the questioner opens the question block by asking a question of a single candidate or of all candidates, depending upon the question block.

The advantage of this question introduction approach is that it adds variety to the standard question block format and injects citizen input into the question set-up.

Debate Program Introductory and Closing Sequences:

- *Opening Segment*
    Moderator introduction
    Welcomes audience
    Introduces the questioners
    Introduces candidates
    Explains rules
    Reads statement from invited candidate(s) who did not accept invitation
    Introduces opening statements

    - *Moderator directs Candidate A to open*
    - *Candidate A opens*
    - *Moderator directs Candidate B to open*
    - *Candidate B opens*

- *Closing Segment*
    Moderator directs Candidate B to give closing statement
    Candidate B closes
    Moderator directs Candidate A to give closing statement
    Candidate A closes
    Moderator wrap-up

CHAPTER 5

Nationwide Poll: What Voters Think About Candidate Debates

By Ronald A. Faucheux

D ebates in political campaigns are one of the most important sources of information for voters about candidates. Though face-to-face confrontations play a major strategic role in many competitive elections, little attention has been given to what voters think of them, especially in contests below the presidential level.

To get a handle on voter attitudes about political debates, The Pew Charitable Trusts funded the Debate Advisory Standards Project, sponsored through the Center for American Politics and Citizenship at the University of Maryland. The purpose of the project is to study non-presidential political debates and to develop a series of guidelines for sponsoring groups and news organizations to use. A key part of the project has been assessing public opinion.

The following are key findings developed from a nationwide poll of voters. This survey was based on a sample of 1,000 registered voters across the United States with a margin of error of +/- 4%. It was conducted Feb. 22 to 24, 2002. Telephone interviewing services were provided by Communications Center Inc.

Where Do Voters Get Information About Candidates?

KEY FINDING: Candidate debates, which cost

campaigns little or nothing in terms of dollars, are preferred by voters as an information source over the candidates' own ads, which consume a majority of most major campaign budgets, by over a 7-to-1 ratio.

Results from this question provide a context for studying political campaign debates as a source of information for voters. Clearly, based on these results, debates rate as a significant source of such information. Face-to-face candidate encounters are a major factor in the political campaign process.

Voters say the source of "the best, most useful information" about political candidates is TV news shows (24%), newspaper articles (24%) and candidate debates (20%). These top three sources rated far above radio news shows (8%), campaign speeches (6%), news magazines (6%), the candidates' own advertisements (3%), Web sites sponsored by news organizations (2%) and the candidates' own Web sites (1%).

Gender differences were most apparent involving radio news shows (10% of men vs. 6% of women) and candidate debates (23% of women vs. 16% of men).

The age cohort that rated TV news shows the highest were those voters under age 25 (33%); the lowest was the 55-64 age cohort (24%).

Educational attainment is a strong predictor of voters' preferred source of candidate information. TV news shows are by far more important for voters with the least education (12 years of schooling or less, 38%) as opposed to those with the most (16 years of schooling or more, 18%). Twenty-two percent of voters with 13 years or more of education selected campaign debates while only 14 percent of those with 12 years of schooling or less did so. Twenty-nine percent of voters with 16 years of education or more selected newspaper articles while 20 percent of those with 12 years or less did so.

Candidate debates do best among middle-aged voters (age 35-64, 22%) and least well among the youngest voters (under age 25, 15%) and the oldest voters (over age 65, 16%).

Democrats think slightly less of candidate debates than do

Republicans (17% vs. 21%).

Black voters are much more reliant on TV news shows (37%) than on newspaper articles (15%) and debates (15%), and prefer campaign speeches (10%) more than do white electors (6%).

Republicans and independents were more likely to select Web sites sponsored by news organizations (3%) than were Democrats (1%). Democrats and independents put a little more stock in newspaper articles than do Republicans (25% and 26% vs. 21%).

Radio news shows are most popular in the Northeast (11%) and least popular in the South (5%).

Newspaper articles were selected by older voters (over age 65, 25%) more often than by younger voters (age 25-29, 11%).

The youngest voter cohort (under 25) considers campaign speeches to be more important than does the oldest voter cohort (over 65), 12% to 6%. (Perhaps, this statistic undermines the notion that campaign speechmaking is an "old-fashioned" technique.)

It should be noted that many political media consultants discount poll questions such as this one as they relate to measuring the impact of campaign advertisements. They argue that while voters may not honestly regard candidate-sponsored ads as an important information source, election tracking polls and considerable anecdotal evidence indicate that these ads have more impact on moving public opinion than the voters actually realize.

Do Voters Want More Debates?

KEY FINDING: Voters who think there should be more debates outnumber those who think there should be fewer debates by nearly a 4-to-1 ratio (35% to 9%).

A majority of the electorate (54%) thinks there is already about the right amount of candidate debates.

Independents (39%) and Democrats (38%) favor more

debates to a greater degree than do Republicans (30%); more men (39%) than women (31%) do, too.

Voters in the Northeast were most inclined to say they want more debates (41%) while voters in the South were the least inclined (32%).

Voters aged 45-55 were most likely to want more debates (41%) while voters over 65 were least likely (26%).

Interestingly, suburban voters want more debates (40%) to a greater extent than do rural and small town voters (31%).

Choosing the more debates option was directly related to educational attainment: 29% of voters with 12 years of schooling or less compared to 37% with 13-16 years of schooling and 40% with 16 years or more of schooling.

Are Candidate Debates Helpful?

KEY FINDING: The higher the office, the more helpful voters say debates are in making the voting decision. However, strong majorities of voters say debates are helpful at every office level – national, statewide, district and local.

Over three-fourths (76%) of voters said political candidate debates are either very helpful or somewhat helpful in deciding how they will vote in elections for president. That compares with 70% who said so for debates in elections for major statewide offices such as governor or U.S. senator and 59% who said so in elections for district and local offices such as the U.S. House, the state legislature, mayor or city and county council.

Voters under age 25 were the strongest in their belief that presidential debates are very helpful or somewhat helpful (82%) while voters over 65 were weakest (64%) in such a belief. Interestingly, the variance between the youngest and the oldest age cohorts virtually disappears when debates for statewide offices are measured (62% vs. 61%), but re-emerges somewhat when debates for district and local offices are measured (64% vs. 55%).

How Often Should Candidates Debate?

KEY FINDING: While an overwhelming majority of voters think candidates should have multiple debates during an election, and while most voters say the higher the office the more debates should be held, the bulk of the electorate is ready to limit the number of such encounters to four or fewer.

In major statewide elections:

Eighty-three percent of the voters polled think there should be multiple debates while 11% said one debate and 4% said no debates. Of the sample polled, 39% wanted three or four debates in gubernatorial and U.S. Senate races, 27% said two debates, 14% preferred five to 10 debates and 3% suggested more than 10 debates.

In district and local elections:

Sixty-two percent of the voters polled think there should be multiple debates while 23% said one debate and 12% said no debates. Of the sample polled, 26% wanted two debates in these downballot races, 25% said three or four debates, 8% preferred five to 10 debates and 3% suggested more than 10 debates.

How Many Debates Will Voters Watch?

KEY FINDING: Regardless of the number of debates each voter thinks should be held, a high proportion of voters would be willing to watch most or all of them.

In major statewide elections:

• Of those voters who said major statewide candidates should debate three times or more, 74% said they would watch all of them or most of them, 23% said they would watch a few of them and only 2% said they would view none of them.

• Of those voters who said major statewide candidates should debate two times, 73% said they would watch both of them, 23% said they would watch one of them and only 3% said they would view none of them.

• Of those voters who said major statewide candidates should debate one time, 87% said they would be willing to watch the debate and 12% said they would not watch it.

In district and local elections:

• Of those voters who said district and local candidates should debate three times or more, 64% said they would watch all of them or most of them, 30% said they would watch a few of them and only 4% said they would view none of them.

• Of those voters who said district and local candidates should debate two times, 71% said they would watch both of them, 21% said they would watch one of them and only 7% said they would view none of them.

• Of those voters who said district and local candidates should debate one time, 83% said they would be willing to watch the debate and 12% said they would not watch it.

Presumably, voters who say they want debates held but are not willing to watch still believe it's important for *other* voters to watch these debates or that post-debate news coverage is an adequate substitute to watching the full debates.

Why Voters Think Debates Are Important

KEY FINDING: Voters believe political debates are important because they give them a chance to find out where candidates stand on the issues and how the candidates differ.

Of those voters polled, 89% say political debates are important because they give voters a chance to learn where the candidates stand on the issues, while 81% say debates are important because they help voters get a personal sense of who the candidates are as people. Also, 89% say debates are important because they give voters a chance to determine the differences between candidates.

An overwhelming majority of voters (84%) reject the notion that political debates are a waste of time because most of the candidates don't have anything important to say.

What Do Voters Think About Debate Rules?

KEY FINDING: Voters believe debate rules should give candidates more time to discuss their views on complex issues.

Most voters (71%) think debates would be better if the rules would give candidates more time to explain their views on complex issues. This is a particularly prevalent point of view among voters under 30 (82%), voters with 12 years or less of schooling (78%), blacks (77%), men (75%) and the South (74%).

What Impact Does a Candidate's Refusal to Debate Have on How Voters Vote?

KEY FINDING: Candidates who refuse to debate do so at substantial risk.

A solid 57% majority of survey respondents said they would be less likely to vote for a major candidate for governor or U.S. senator if that candidate refused to debate, 3% said more likely and 37% said it would make no difference.

The responses were similar in races for district and local offices: 55% say less likely, 2% say more likely and 41% say it would make no difference.

Refusing to debate in major statewide elections is especially harmful to candidates among the 30- to 44-year-old age cohort; nearly 70% of those voters say they would be less likely to vote for such a candidate. That age cohort demonstrated a similar, though slightly less pronounced, propensity as it applied to candidates in elections for district and local offices (66%).

What Role Can the Internet Play in Candidate Debates?

KEY FINDING: There is a large pool of voters

nationwide who have expressed a willingness to participate online in political debates.

About 38% of the voters sampled expressed some willingness to participate in a political debate conducted entirely on the Internet by asking questions through e-mail: 8% said they would be very likely to participate, 13% said somewhat likely and 17% said only slightly likely. Sixty-two percent said they were not likely at all to participate.

Although the percentage of voters who said they were very likely to participate seems small, it translates into a large number of voters in actual elections.

For example, in a congressional district with 300,000 registered voters, 8% translates to 24,000 voters – a substantial number of people – who said they would be very likely to participate in an online debate.

In a statewide election with 2 million registered voters, for instance, 8% translates to 160,000 people – a large pool from which to draw possible participants for such a forum.

There was a large difference between how voters reacted to participating in a completely online debate and how they reacted to participating in using the Internet to vote on the questions that will be asked of candidates in a televised debate. This result reinforces the idea that the Internet is most powerful and most useful in politics when it is integrated with other media.

Sixty-three percent of voters expressed some willingness to go online and have their say on which questions would be asked in a televised debate.

Of the respondents surveyed, 23% said they would be very likely to go to an Internet Web site and vote on questions to be asked of the candidates in an upcoming debate on television, 28% said somewhat likely, 13% said only slightly likely and 37% said not likely at all.

Again, the proportion of those very likely to participate translates into big numbers in actual elections – 69,000 in a congressional district with 300,000 voters and 460,000 in a state with 2 million voters.

Groups that most often said they would be very likely to

vote on TV debate questions via the Internet are voters under 25 (28%), voters 45-54 (28%) and voters who live in cities with over a million population (31%). Voters with at least some college education expressed greater willingness to participate than those without any college schooling (26% vs. 15%).

In the survey, 34% of the sample reported that they have used the Internet to find some type of political information, such as to register to vote, information about an election or campaign or about political issues and organizations. Independents (36%) and Republicans (35%) reported more Internet political usage than Democrats (31%); whites (34%) more than blacks (28%); men (40%) more than women (28%); the West (38%) more than any other region; voters under age 25 (54%) more than any other age cohort; suburban voters (42%) more than big city (36%), small city (37%), small town (28%) and rural voters (27%); and voters with graduate or professional degrees (51%) more than those with college degrees (39%), some college (32%), high school or vo-tech graduates (22%) and less than high school (12%).

Who Should Ask the Questions in a Debate?

KEY FINDING: There is strong sentiment that average citizens should play a role in candidate debates.

Most voters believe that average citizens should ask the questions in debates. Given a choice of three formats – average citizens asking the questions, journalists and reporters asking the questions, and the candidates asking the questions of one another – nearly half the sample (49%) selected average citizens, while 23% selected journalists and reporters, and 11% selected candidates. In addition, 7% proffered a combination of average citizens and journalists, 4% said a combination of average citizens and candidates, and 2% said a combination of journalists and candidates.

In total, six-of-10 voters sampled want average citizens to play a role in the debate questioning process.

The demographic groups who most favored average citizen participation were: voters 30-34 (59%), rural voters (57%), independents (55%), voters with some college (55%), voters under 25 (54%) and women (53%).

Should Third-Party Candidates Be Included?

KEY FINDING: Voters are much more likely to include non-major party candidates in debates than to exclude them.

One of the stickiest issues of staging political candidate debates in general elections is whether to include non-major party candidates, such as nominees of the Libertarian Party, the Green Party, the Natural Law Party and the Reform Party.

A majority of the voters surveyed (53%) said candidates from these parties should always be included in general election debates.

In addition, 39% think third-party candidates should only be included if they have a reasonable chance to win the election.

In total, nearly nine-of-10 voters think non-major third-party candidates should have at least some access to candidate debates.

Only one-out-of-20 voters (5%) said flatly that non-major party candidates should never be included.

Voters under 30 (61%) and independents (59%) are the two groups most likely to want non-major party candidates to always be included in debates.

What Voters Want Out of Debates

KEY FINDING: When it comes to candidate debates, voters indicate substance is more important than style.

Voters were asked about how they judge candidate performance in political debates.

The two factors that stood out were the candidates'

knowledge of the issues and the candidates' positions on the issues. These two factors were selected as very important by 92% and 85% of the respondents polled, respectively.

The candidates' ability to keep cool and calm was cited by 70% of the sample as being very important. That compares to 58% who said the candidates' speaking ability was very important.

Interestingly, only 26% said the candidates' physical appearance was very important and only 16% said the candidates' willingness to attack one another was very important in how they judge candidate debates.

Voters seem to have an instinct for separating style from substance.

What Role Did Debates Play in the 2000 Presidential Election?

KEY FINDING: Many voters said the 2000 presidential election debates played an important role in how they ultimately voted.

Nearly two-thirds of the voters polled say presidential debates played an important role in how they ultimately voted in the 2000 election. Of those, 29% said presidential debates were very important and another 37% said they were somewhat important in their balloting choice. Only 22% said the debates were not important at all to their vote.

Based on these survey results, it can be argued that the debates likely played an important role in that exceptionally close national election.

CHAPTER 6

Focus Group Findings: Voters on Debates

By Mark Watts

In February 2002, Abacus Associates conducted two focus groups with likely voters in Secaucus, N.J., and Richmond, Va. Media analyst Allen Churchill assisted in the effort. The focus groups aimed to assess public opinion toward candidate debates and how debates should be improved.

Are Debates Informative?

Participants in both focus groups overwhelmingly believe debates deliver important information about candidates – information necessary for making informed decisions when choosing a candidate. Participants also believe that debates offer information they cannot find anywhere else. Furthermore, while participants rely in varying degrees on newspapers, talk radio and mailings to their homes for information, all participants say they receive some information from debates and that debates play a major role in their decisions.

Despite participants' beliefs that debates provide important information, only a few watch debates for statewide or local office. Clearly, statewide and local debates need to be made more accessible and visible to voters. Local television and radio must cover state and local debates, and the news media, candidates, parties and debate sponsors need to do a better job publicizing debates.

In both Virginia and New Jersey, participants believe candidates should debate their opponents during the campaign. When candidates do not debate opponents, voters question their ability to hold higher office. In their view, the only reason a candidate would choose not to debate is to hide a significant failure.

What Voters Like About Debates

Participants' views about what they wanted to see in debates were strikingly similar – both within each group and across the two. While participants were not in absolute agreement about desirable and undesirable debate characteristics, their responses came unusually close to unanimity. Indeed, with respect to each individual debate characteristic discussed here, no more than two participants departed from the majority view. As a consequence, neither focus group saw much discussion of what characteristics a debate should have. Disagreement centered on how to produce better debates.

Participants value debates for giving them an opportunity to see and hear candidates free of media filtering and outside the choreographed and controlled settings of ads and speeches. They value debates because they are – at least in their ideal form – spontaneous, unscripted and honest.

I like that they are live . . . not rehearsed. Or supposedly it's not rehearsed . . . . It shows more of their natural selves in that venue than like a commercial where it puts them in a casual shirt which is supposed to be "natural."(Virginia female)

That's really learning about the candidate – when these two people are standing there, and they just have to be themselves because it's a live audience and they know everybody is watching them . . . .This isn't just a TV camera being recorded to be edited, this is them. I think that's the best way to find out about somebody. (New Jersey female)

It shows the candidates' ability to go beyond the script. (New

Jersey male)

According to participants, debates go deeper into the issues, show more of the candidates' knowledge of the issues and address a wider range of issues than do other campaign elements. Because the debates are unscripted, participants feel they provide a better sense of how well the candidates understand the issues than do stump speeches or campaign ads. A strong Democrat and Gore supporter from New Jersey offered the following example: He had heard from the media that George W. Bush was a lightweight on the issues, but he learned from the debates that Bush actually had a good grasp of the issues.

They have to explain how they are going to do it . . . . [Y]ou really get a sense of who understands and who has done his home-work. So you get to know who is knowledgeable on the issues. (New Jersey female)

Are they giving you a full deal about what they are cam-paigning about? A lot in their advertisement they will just cut it all so far, but when they are out at the media and they know the audience and the TVs are looking at them, they tend to give a better answer or a clearer answer. (New Jersey male)

It brings the issues to the forefront . . . and it can clear up a lot of things that you might read in the paper here and there or catch on the news, but I think most of the issues are going to be addressed. (Virginia male)

Participants also believe debates show the candidates' capacity for quick thinking and their ability to handle pres-sure – important character traits in the eyes of many voters.

They are under a lot of pressure, and I like to see how they handle the pressure and see what their strength and character is. (New Jersey female)

How they answer a question – especially in the presidential election? If this guy can't handle the pressure of rebutting a question thrown at him I mean . . . how is he going to stand up in a national crisis? (Virginia male)

Beyond exposing the candidates' ability to handle pressure, participants feel debates show the candidate "as a person." For these participants, debates reveal candidates' characters, personalities and styles, traits rarely exposed in more controlled environments. A number of participants also cite "body language" as an important source of information during debates.

I think it is also a good place to kind of judge what you think their character is. How straightforward they are when they answer the question or if they try to dance around. (Virginia female)

I like to watch body language during the debate because body language tells you a lot more than the words that they are speaking because they can speak an awful lot of words but sometimes a little movement shows you something different. (New Jersey female)

You can see facial expressions, body language. If they are stammering or if they have a good command of what they are responding to and you get a good idea of how they react under pressure. If their body starts to shift you can tell somebody is getting nervous. If they start to move around or if they are at a loss for words. (New Jersey male)

Finally, debates also are valued for their fairness, primarily because they give candidates an equal chance to be heard. Most participants believe minor party candidates should be included in debates and that moderators should be as neutral as possible – with many expressing the belief that most journalists are insufficiently neutral.

*The structure tries to be evenhanded. They go out of their way .
. . to make certain that the structure does not benefit anyone. (New
Jersey male)*

*I like the opportunity for rebuttal. The one thing that you don't
get from 30-second spot ads is what the other side has to say. I think
rebuttal is an important aspect. (Virginia male)*

What participants say they value in debates is, in large part,
an indictment of the rest of campaigns. Many say debates are
important because they are one of the few times, if not the
only time, they receive "real" information. Campaign advertisements and media news coverage of campaigns provide
extremely filtered, choreographed and scripted presentations
of the candidates. Voters feel advertisements and news coverage do not provide opportunities to see candidates for who
they really are and do not provide enough information to evaluate candidates' knowledge and positions on all issues.
Participants value debates because candidates must let down
their protective guards and speak and act outside the control of
their handlers.

What Voters Dislike About Debates

When participants criticize debates, it is often for their failure to live up to their potential. Participants object to candidates' giving rehearsed and simplistic canned responses and
avoiding difficult questions or questions that might take them
off message. They especially dislike debate formats with brief
response periods or no opportunity for follow-up questions
because these formats allow candidates to avoid answering
questions. Finally, participants object to moderators' "softball" questions that allow candidates to give scripted answers.

*Often it is still too short. I say on one hand they have to go by
the script but it often starts that it is not quite sound biting where
they could be structured enough to fill that minute and a half. If*

they really had to fill up four minutes on a subject ... it could go deeper and it doesn't so it is somewhere between the sound biting, you know they had to be an actor . . . .(New Jersey male)

These so-called . . . panel of reporters down here who throw softball questions at the candidates. They stink; I hate them. ... [A]s an observer it looks like it is scripted. (Virginia male)

I worry about the aspect of the whole thing being too staged. I think that during the last presidential debates that we saw what was happening to Gore because Gore was changing his demeanor with each debate so I felt like he was being over-advised by ... the people that advise him. ... Therefore, we didn't find out who Gore was, we found out who Gore wasn't. (New Jersey female)

With the exception of length of response period and the opportunity for follow-up questions, participants in New Jersey rarely mentioned specific formats when they criticized debates. However, in Virginia, several participants mentioned a dislike for debates that are restricted to the two main parties. Excluding minor party candidates violated participants' sense of fairness, an attribute they valued in debates.

...[O]nly two political candidates can be part of debates – at least for the presidency – and I would like to see other groups, even though they are not necessarily representing a lot of people. I would really like to get input from these other groups. I may not agree with them. (Virginia female)

I think from congressional to local to presidential races that all the candidates, I don't care who [they] are, they should be heard. (Virginia male)

Participants in both states agreed that although including many candidates might make debates more difficult, minor party candidates should be included – in both presidential and lower-level races – for the sake of fairness. However, when probed on this issue, participants agreed that the number of candidates needed to be limited to make debates work-able. Most accepted four candidates as an appropriate limit. However, participants could not come up with a way to decide who should be included or excluded.

A number of participants in the Virginia focus group objected to candidates' breaking the rules by going over their allotted time or failing to answer questions. Most believed that exceeding time limits should be punished through an award of extra time to the offending candidate's opponent. With respect to failure to answer questions, most opposed punishment. Participants believed that the moderator should note that the question had not been answered and pose the question again. Participants opposed further punishment based on their belief that the damage to a candidate's image caused by question-avoidance is punishment enough.

In both states – though this view was expressed much more strongly in New Jersey – participants object to candi-dates' "going negative." Complaints about negative cam-paigning, of course, are a consistent feature of public com-ment on contemporary politics, whether attacks on oppo-nents appear in media coverage, advertising or debates. Our participants see negative attacks as a frequent and thorough-ly distasteful feature of debates.

I dislike what has happened, like backstabbing....Making negative remarks about the candidate, that is not the issue here. It is a debate. I'm sticking to what I believe in and you are stick-ing to what you believe in. It is not here for me to put you down. It is for me to say what I am going to do in a positive way, not to say what is negative about you. (New Jersey female)

...[W]hen they get into digging into people's past and bring-ing up things that don't pertain . . . . You are there to study the issues and you are there to do what you have to do ... you don't need the mudslinging and the name calling, and let's be honest everybody is grown up here. (New Jersey male)

Although participants objected strenuously to negative

attacks, no one came up with a way to eliminate them from debates. They identified no format or rule of debate that led to more negative attacks. Some participants did mention the round table conversation as a more civil format. However, they mentioned this preference only after seeing a clip from the 2000 Cheney-Lieberman vice presidential debate, which was particularly civil and in a round table conversation set style. Their response may have been different had they seen the Gore-Perot NAFTA debate, which was a debate staged during a TV talk show but decidedly less civil. Clearly the tone of a debate is driven much more by the participating candidates than by format. However, a moderator can set the tone to some extent.

Participants also say they dislike debates with excessive drama and a lack of civility or control. Although these attributes might make debates entertaining or "good television" and are often focused on by pundits and journalists, participants – with only a few exceptions – dislike them. Participants particularly dislike debates that devolve into disorderly arguments.

[The] thing that I don't like about it is the dramatics....[some candidates] use [a] question as a campaigning tool rather than really addressing the issue. (Virginia male)

...[D]uring a rebuttal sometimes they seem like there is just an argument that starts and nobody gets to finish their point because they are both screaming. Sometimes they just can't seem to get their point across. (Virginia female)

Some participants criticize debates for their failure to show which candidate would be the best leader. They feel that candidates who might be great leaders are not necessarily great debaters and candidates who might be great debaters are not necessarily great leaders.

Sometimes the more skilled debater or the more charming personality wins out over substance. (New Jersey female)

...[D]ebates by their nature can rule out certain types of candidates. People that are not particularly photogenic or who are not as quick on their feet ... I can't help but wonder who we are self-limiting by debates. (Virginia male)

This criticism contradicts the argument that debates are good because they reveal the candidates' knowledge of and position on the issues, the candidates' personality, and the candidates' ability to handle pressure – all perceived as important measures of leadership and less available to voters outside of debates. Like the criticism that debates are too scripted or too negative, this complaint applies not just to debates but to all information voters receive during campaigns, as voters routinely complain that what makes a good candidate does not necessarily make a good leader.

Choosing Debate Formats

The relatively high level of consensus regarding the desirable and undesirable characteristics of debates breaks down when participants are asked about specific debate formats. Because participants do not usually identify format as the determining factor in what makes a debate good or bad, they rarely express a causal relationship such as "I like debates to be spontaneous, so debates should be formatted _____ way to improve spontaneity." Although they clearly know what they value about debates, their comments on formats are based more on immediate "call-it-as-I-see-it" reactions than on sophisticated analysis.

However, the major reason consensus breaks down over formats is that certain formats tend to engender both positive and negative debate characteristics. For instance, a debate format that maximizes spontaneity and reality also may be prone to negative attacks and disorder. Similarly, an orderly format with minimal interaction (and thus minimal attacks) may make a debate seem overly controlled and scripted – lacking the spontaneity and authenticity that make debates important and distinctive sources of information. Character and personality may be revealed more clearly in a free-flowing, "attack-prone" debate style and be less visible in a more orderly, formal style. Furthermore, when moderators ask "hard" follow-up questions that force candidates to address issues fully, it becomes more difficult to prevent negative attacks and maintain order and a sense of fairness.

The following exchange among three participants in the Virginia focus group provides a good example of how certain formats demonstrate both positive and negative debate characteristics:

Female: As far as them asking each other questions, the only part I don't like about it is you can get into a lot of arguments and tend to be critical of one another . . . .It still goes back to making that person look bad . . . .So that is the part I don't like.

Male: But you know that in itself is very critical because again you are seeing these two people acting under pressure and you know the guy who handles a difficult situation coolly and more professionally, you see that.

These three participants were discussing the classic debate structure in which debaters ask each other questions. This format is often valued as the best and truest form of debate by communication and political scholars. It is also a format that all participants say they have never seen used in American campaigns.

Participants are very divided over whether it is a good format. As the exchange above demonstrates, participants worry that the format may violate the goal of fairness or exacerbate the problem of negative attacks. However, at least one participant praises the format for providing more opportunity to see candidates handle pressure. Participants tend to disagree over formats because they can see how any particular format might contradict what they value about debates. This disagreement occurs despite the fact that most participants value the same characteristics of debates.

Despite their disagreements over debate formats, participants did support a few common standards. Participants would like to be able to see both candidates simultaneously on the television screen; they especially like formats in which the candidates stand or sit near each other. They believe audiences should not be allowed to react to the candidates – no cheering, clapping, or show of support for one side or the other should be permitted. Debate audiences should be neutral, undecided and nonpartisan and/or should be under strict rules of silence.

Most participants prefer one moderator to a panel of moderators. Moderators should be neutral, fair and maintain control over the debate. They should ask hard questions, press the candidates when they give evasive or simplistic responses, repeat questions if they are not answered and penalize candidates if they go over their allotted time. Moderators should not pose questions about personal attacks that have been made in the campaign. To the greatest degree possible, the same questions should be posed to all candidates. Candidates should not be able to limit the questions, nor should they be allowed to see the questions beforehand.

Making Debates Useful for Voters

According to participants, debates should provide information – not entertainment. However, although participants say they value information and a diversity of candidates in debates, they do not seek information about a diversity of offices. Participants tend to watch only presidential and vice presidential debates and rarely seek out debates for state and local offices, despite the information those debates could provide.

Increasing viewership is likely to result from increasing the accessibility of and publicity about debates and creating debate formats that provide voters with an informative, unscripted, civil, issue-oriented discussion – a discussion that provides honest insight into the positions, knowledge, character and personality of the candidates.

Although political "debate" television shows featuring ideologues and pundits screaming at each other are considered entertaining and may result in more viewers than a more civil and informative format, these shows are designed for political junkies and political partisans. They are not designed to inform the nonpartisan, less politically informed or undecided voter.

Voters who meet this definition do not want debates to be entertaining screaming contests. They want clear, honest information to help them make decisions. Based on the comments made by participants in these focus groups, debates should be as informative, unscripted, fair and issue-oriented as possible and candidates should be held accountable for giving honest, straightforward answers. Most importantly, debates (and candidates) should maintain a civil tone. Debates that meet these goals will attract more viewers because they give voters the types of information voters feel they need for choosing their candidate.

CHAPTER 7

Using the Internet in Sponsoring Candidate Debates

By Michael Cornfield

This chapter outlines a seven-step process to harness the Internet to enhance public debates by candidates for office. It also recommends other possible uses of the new medium in one of this nation's most cherished democratic rituals.

Debates are special events in U.S. campaigns for public office in three respects: The candidates appear together, in a format that none of them controls, and the results are more or less available to all who desire to know about them. The Internet can enrich debates on each count, at very low cost. It can expand the number of candidates who participate. It can host longer and more intricate interactions. And it can disseminate more results to more people. Clearly, then, the Internet should be part of the media mix through which debates are promoted, staged, discussed and preserved.

But how can this be done to maximize fidelity to the contradictory purposes that campaign debates embody? On the one hand, debates are supposed to generate serious content about the candidates' political abilities and issue positions.

Prospective voters need to come away from a debate with a better sense of which candidate is better prepared for the decision-making job, and which candidate is likeliest to make decisions that agree with the voters' individual views. (Of course, these two voter criteria may conflict. The person who appears better suited to the job may hold policy views contrary to the voter's. But no one ever said being a citizen is easy.)

On the other hand, debates should be lively enough to grab and hold popular interest. Otherwise, enough people won't be moved to pay attention, to vote on Election Day and to vote with their impressions of the debates in mind. If those three things don't happen in sufficient numbers, then the debates are incidental to the election result, regardless of their substantiality. A substantive debate with a tiny audience is the political equivalent of the tree falling in the empty forest.

Debate sponsors must therefore find a way to make a policy discussion attract a crowd. Commercial television normally attempts to meet this challenge by casting well-known and exhibitionist personalities as the debaters and moderators: the late "Politically Incorrect," "Crossfire," "Hardball," the Sunday morning public affairs shows, etc. But debate sponsors, especially beneath the presidential level, are denied this option. Even when state and local candidates possess a modicum of celebrity appeal or reputation, their obligations to the blocs in their electoral coalitions constrain their performances. Whereas television personalities can court giving offense to an interest group or party, candidates for office must avoid it. Besides, entertainment values seem inappropriate to an event in which the power to make important decisions about other people's lives is at stake.

As the Debate Advisory Standards Project focus groups indicated (see Chapter 6), debate viewers "particularly dislike debates that devolve into disorderly arguments." What entertainment there is in a candidate debate ought to emerge as a natural byproduct of a civil and serious approach. Comic relief is fine; playing for laughs is not.

Staging a successful debate in terms of what our political system requires of campaigns and elections is thus a very tall order. But the Internet is quite a ladder.

Three Principles

The Internet has been part of American politics since the early 1990s. This has been a period of scarce, but highly visible and much discussed, experimentation in online politics.

Two lessons stand out from the efforts of the "dot-pols." First, the Internet is best deployed in combination with, not as a replacement for or replication of, the "offline" media of contemporary politics: face-to-face meetings, display graphics, direct mail, telephone, radio, television and print (the last three via both paid advertisements and news coverage "earned" through good press relations).

The Internet can mimic and reproduce political communication in these older media. That versatility lured some into believing that all media would converge into the Internet. However, the tremendous volume of messages available online at any moment – along with the crucial fact that the receiver, not the sender, controls what is seen, when and for how long – means that the finest online communication will go unnoticed by most people unless it is publicized offline, both before and after. Before, to gain the largest real-time audience; after, so that more of those who missed the live event can witness it through archived information.

An online debate, like any other online event, is no "Field of Dreams." People will come only through extensive coordinated efforts to get them there. The byword for this lesson within the dot-pol community is integration. Online and offline communications should be coordinated to be effective.

The second lesson for debate sponsors is that the people who choose to access an online debate (live or later; wholly or in part) will do so with a variety of technical and civic capabilities. A civic divide cuts at right angles to the digital divide, creating four categories of people for whom a debate must be made legible in order to maximize its audience, its impact and the equality of its dissemination.

The best-known categorical pair are: (A) the double "haves," or "netizens" as one early and enthusiastic observer tagged them, the people with broadband connections and a penchant for news and voting, and (B) the double "have-nots," people who have yet to connect to the Net, and live their lives estranged from conventional politics. But there are also: (C) frequent and sophisticated Net users who lack the motivation to click into public affairs, many of whom are young, and (D) veteran political activists who, for one reason or another, shy away from the Web and e-mail, and wouldn't be caught dead text messaging.

The social fact of variegated access makes versioning an imperative in online political communication. For example, as soon as an (integrated) publicity campaign entices people to check out the online interface of a debate (generally, a Web page), they had better see a number of ways by which they can take the next step and reach the contents they want to examine.

Group A types will be able and eager to search a database of debate videoclips by keyword.

Group C types might benefit from a flashy highlight package that concludes with a point-and-click index to the issues behind the dramatic confrontations.

Debate organizers must assure that there be a multipath navigational system that encourages sophisticates and novices, in both the technical and civic senses of those terms, to locate debate material likely to be of interest to them.

Integration and versioning are crucial for any application of the Internet to public affairs; without them, people will not attend in sufficient numbers and time to warrant the effort. The brief history of online debates to date yields a third, more specific and complicated lesson, one that applies to debates offline as well: Organizers must take care to construct a system of interlocking incentives that attracts journalists and candidates as well as citizens.

Journalists, not just sponsors, must be part of online debates, to certify their impartiality and draw an audience broader than the supporters for one candidate. Candidates, not just campaign surrogates, must be involved, to certify a debate's authenticity and excite the audience. Citizens, like journalists and candidates, will participate to the extent that they think the other two groups will. So the trick is to set up a debate that appeals to the three groupings simultaneously, and builds momentum for the event through publicity for their increasing commitments.

How can this be done? Research conducted for the Markle Foundation, the organizers of the civic site Web, White, and Blue's "Rolling Cyber-Debate" among seven presidential candidates in 2000, confirmed that:

• Journalists want unrehearsed debate segments among top candidates.

• Candidates want unfiltered segments to get campaign-framed versions of their messages directly to voters.

• Citizens want background information as well as the fore-grounded segments, available where and when they want it.

The Rolling Cyber-Debate met two of the three incentives in its 37 days of operation. Candidates were allotted space for a message of the day on the topic and in the multimedia format of their choosing. Citizens were able to look at any and all parts of the entire debate to date, as well as link to civic education and voter registration sites. What's more, because the debate contents were carried through a syndicated network of 17 large Internet sites, nearly 90 percent of Americans online were likely to run across at least a link to the event in their normal Net accessing – and candidates knew that the debate had this huge potential reach.

Including major news media sites in the network provided an incentive for journalists to pay attention, as well. However, the Rolling Cyber-Debate lacked a live interactive segment, which reduced its news value and, thereby, its appeal to candidates and citizens.

Seven-Step Process

The debate process outlined in this section attempts to incorporate these principles and early lessons. It integrates the Internet with offline publicity and a live and unscripted broadcast. It has roles for experts and amateurs in both technology and politics. It allows participating candidates to contribute unedited material. And it provides the news media with a sustained and multifaceted role: to encourage journalistic involvement as guides to, narrators of and unofficial scorekeepers for the process, as well as the rights to carry portions of the debates exclusively from their own sites, all meant to boost traffic to their political sections.

Before the debate:

1. Residents of the election jurisdiction submit questions for the debate by e-mail, Web forms and offline channels. As a practical matter, outsiders will be able to submit questions, too. They may be screened somewhat by requiring submitters to enter an address. What matters, however, is not the purity of the submitting pool, but the excitement built by the process, and the variety of questions generated.

2. Debate sponsors filter the questions, organize them by topic, and post them online and in other public outlets. This weeds out frivolous, obscene, duplicative, loaded, unclear and otherwise undesirable questions. It also gives the campaigns a preview of the likely topics to be covered, enabling candidates to give complete, well-organized responses. The desired result is a question/topic: a well-phrased question designed to elicit a candidate issue position on a topic pertinent to the electorate.

3. Visitors to the debate Web site rank the filtered question/topics, and a running tabulation displays the top 10 questions for the debate. This vote can be advisory, for sheer publicity, or it can yield several question/topics that will actually be asked during the debate. Again, the fact that the rankings will not be a representative sample of the electorate matters less than the interest drummed up by an ongoing posting of the top questions. Major League Baseball mounted something akin to this step for the 2002 All-Star Game; the 30th and final position on each league's roster was filled by fans, who voted online from a choice of five players.

One of the great revelations of the 1992 presidential debates was how good live questions from citizens can be. To increase participation and publicity, the Internet should serve as a main conduit (but not an exclusive one) to collect questions that might be posed to candidates during a debate. Professional communicators should screen and shape the submitted questions, and – a feature uniquely feasible through the Net – citizens who reside in the area that the candidates are vying to represent should rate the filtered questions.

Steven Clift of Minnesota E-Democracy, who may have

more experience with online debates than anyone, recommends that the lead-up period be as long as possible. Citizens will need to be recruited to participate, and early highlights – tantalizing questions, horse-race ratings results – will help that process.

The questions that emerge as the winners will be extremely difficult for candidates to duck, in as much as they have been created and ratified by the electorate. The nationwide survey conducted for the Debate Advisory Standards Project shows that this phase of the process will not be difficult to sell to the public. As Ron Faucheux reports, "Sixty-three percent of voters expressed some willingness to go online and have their say on which questions would be asked in a televised debate," and "23 percent said they would be very likely" to do so.

During the debate:

4. The posers of top-ranking questions rephrase them live, directing them to the candidate(s) of their choice and staying within the topic as prodded by the moderator. Since a question available in advance will elicit an answer crafted not to offend, the person who poses a Net-approved question must be allowed leeway to rephrase it and direct it without the knowledge of the candidates. Ideally, the originator of the question would deliver the live version, but relying on news media personnel as surrogates may be a more prudent option.

5. As many candidate(s) answer and rebut/comment live as time and the moderator permit.

Although the concept of unmediated public interaction between citizens and candidates has a surface appeal, in practice, it tends to be disastrous: excessively contrived, digressive, ragged or some combination thereof. Direct communication between groups of citizens and candidates should be left to individual campaigns to organize and conduct. Debates require moderators and time limits.

During the debate, the URL of the debate Web site should be visible to television viewers.

After the debate:

Elected officials should be tested in debates for how well they handle people and ideas, but those qualities should not be the only ones tested. The history of broadcast debates is pockmarked by candidates whose reputations were unduly stereotyped by their performances in a key exchange. The Internet can be used to put debate performances in a fuller context. Citizens will benefit from greater access to candidate amplifications, as will journalists, who can annotate them. Candidates should be given anywhere from a day to a week for revisions.

At this post-debate stage, two of the best practices for online campaigning advocated by the Institute for Politics, Democracy & The Internet (www.ipdi.org) come into play. As they expand on their debate performances, candidates should take care to document their positions and to make their case for support through contrasts with their opponents. Americans have come to associate superficiality with sound bites and unfair attacks with "negative ads," but these detrimental aspects of campaigning are not restricted to television. Debate organizers can clamp down on them online and set high standards for the new medium.

6. The campaigns of participating candidates extend, but do not revise, answers and comments as they see fit. The Internet can house transcripts of the candidates' remarks during the debate, additional statements amplifying those remarks, and rebuttals. A matrix format works best, with candidates along one axis and question/topics along the other. Site visitors can thereby see the entire range of comments at a glance then click on particular boxes. For a model, see the dynamic questionnaire known as "D Net," operated by the League of Women Voters, at www.dnet.org.

7. Syndicating news media interpret the debate as they see fit. Online ratings are fine, but no substitute for a scientific poll. Post-debate commentary and data will spill out of the spin rooms, and the more the merrier, for that is a sign of a stimulated public. The news media should be encouraged in advance to design formats for commentary that display the comments alongside links to the debate matrix of transcripts and supplemental statements. In that way, Internet users can readily see

the official debate in a standardized presentation.

The media can be encouraged to conduct instant online polls soliciting public reactions to the debates, including those that ask people to pick a winner. An expensive and flashy option permits debate viewers to react during the debate with the online equivalent of a dial-response meter.

It is important that both of these types of publicity devices be clearly labeled as self-selecting polls that do not reflect a representative sample of the electorate's opinion.

Five Pieces of Extra Advice

Herewith, a few recommendations on other aspects of how debates can make use of the Internet. Although they pertain to the process outlined above, they also stand alone as advice.

• Translate as much of the content as possible into languages with significant minority populations in the election jurisdiction. A good rule of thumb: If the ballot has been translated for legal reasons, then the debate should be, too.

• For elections with many eligible candidates, devise a system of tiered participation. There's no reason to exclude any legitimate candidate from the online sections of the debate discourse. But debate sponsors should exercise the discretionary authority to limit broadcast participation to top candidates, and assign middle- and low-level candidates to less prominent places in the online sections.

Web, White, and Blue 2000 did this quite well. When more than one debate is scheduled, candidates should be allowed to move up or down a tier, but only according to objective criteria (e.g. poll standings) laid out in advance of the first debate.

• Candidates at computer keyboards look phony on television. The better way to assure authenticity is to label exactly which comments come from the candidate (i.e., a transcript of debate remarks) and which come from the campaign (pre- and post-debate statements).

• Webcasts are no substitute today for broadcasts. They cost too much and reach too few. Video highlight packages are much better.

• Budget for technical support staff throughout the process. Help should be available via a "Frequently Asked Questions" Web page, plus a staff ready to field e-mail questions and phone calls.

Measure of Success

While online campaigning has reached the toddler stage, online candidate debating remains in its infancy. This is true at all levels of the election system. In October 2000, while the Rolling Cyber-Debate took place at the presidential level, 44 citizens logged into a debate on the Bismarck (N.D.) Tribune Web site between two candidates for Public Service Commission. (Alas, the Net-accessible record provides no other details.)

In Minnesota, second-tier candidates for the Senate participated in online debates in 2000 (while WCCO Minneapolis posted continuous audience response data), and candidates for mayor of St. Paul took part in an online issues forum in 2001. Early in 2002, research by Christine McConville of the Democracy Online Project disclosed sparse online references, let alone components, to debates among gubernatorial primary candidates in California, Iowa, Massachusetts and even Minnesota.

That sets one bar of success quite low: merely to include the Internet in aspects of a candidate debate. The history of television provides some solace. In comparison with that medium's political maturation, 2002 for the Internet corresponds with television's 1954, the eighth year of availability in the marketplace. On that timeline (and the penetration rates of the media into American society are roughly the same), the Internet analogue to the Kennedy-Nixon debates will not occur until 2008, and the institutionalization of presidential campaign debates lies 22 years ahead, in 2024. One does not have to believe in the hype about "Internet time" moving faster than normal time to hope that online debates develop more quickly than the pace of television.

It is important, in this infancy period, not to be misled into either optimism or pessimism by traffic numbers. For one thing, measuring online traffic is a notoriously ambiguous enterprise. Counts of unique visitors, page views, e-mails to the debate organizers, and other metrics can be generated automatically; the hard part is deriving an acceptable index of penetration from all the data. More importantly, even the contribution of one good question to a candidate debate via the Internet can be a sign of success.

In the final analysis, the quality of a candidate debate depends on its success with the three key groups who must participate.

• First, a debate should test candidates as they will be tested by the offices they seek (or seek to retain).

• Second, it should concentrate the attention of citizens on the choices they can make as voters at the next election.

• Third, it should reward journalists, issue advocates, party officials, and other mediators and organizers for emphasizing the first and second criteria in their execution of the debate.

With these goals in mind, the desires of the American public – as reflected in the poll taken for this project – stand a better chance of being realized in the months, and years, to come.

CHAPTER 8

Debate Sponsorship: An Interview With Janet Brown

Interview by Ronald A. Faucheux

The following interview was conducted with Janet Brown, director of the Commission on Presidential Debates, in her Washington, D.C., office. The topic of the interview was sponsoring candidate debates at the statewide, district and local levels.

Q: What are the most important decisions a media organization or a sponsoring organization has to make in terms of developing an effective debate format?

BROWN: The single most important factor for the sponsoring organization is to decide what will help viewers and listeners get information that will assist them in deciding how to vote. The organization needs to take into account who the audience is, when in the election the debate is taking place, how much is already known about the candidates and therefore what format would be most helpful to voters. Debates should provide citizens with information that is useful in their decision-making process.

Q: In looking at debates, there seems to be six basic formats that are used around the country in statewide, district and local races. Could you tell us what you think are the advantages and disadvantages of each format? Podium set style (where the candidates stand behind podiums)?

BROWN: The podium style is the most traditional. It is the one that has been used most often at the presidential level. There are those who think that it impedes spontaneous conversation because of its formality. While it's helpful to have, perhaps, one podium style debate, using other set styles is a good idea also.

Q: Town meeting style (where the candidates are seated on stools on a stage in front of, or surrounded by, a live audience of citizens)?

BROWN: The obvious advantage is that citizens ask questions of the candidates. The town meeting is popular with the public. They really like questions posed by people that they can identify with. One of the disadvantages is that you don't know what is going to be asked. You may end up with duplication. Questions that are quite narrow may be asked – of interest to the people who ask them, but not necessarily representative of interest across the board.

Q: Round table conversation style (where the candidates are seated right next to one another at a round, oval or square table along with the debate moderator and any questioners)?

BROWN: Round table conversation debates are very good because they encourage conversation. They seem to put candidates at ease. This set style worked very well in 2000 at the presidential level.

Q: Multicandidate panel style (where multiple candidates are seated at a long, rectangular table; and the moderator and any questioners may be seated at a facing table or may be standing at a podium)?

BROWN: A panel of candidates is probably the best way to do it when there are many participants, but try to seat them in a semi-circle or a horseshoe rather than a straight

The Debate Book
line. It facilitates conversation when they can see each other.

Q: Interview show set style (where the candidates are seated in chairs or on a sofa and the host is seated in a chair or behind a small desk)?

BROWN: Talk shows are now so familiar to viewers and listeners that there is an enormous feeling of comfort with them. They are seen as entertaining. By the same token, I think we learned in 2000 that talk shows are not generally perceived by the public as having the seriousness of a debate. They don't match debates in substantive value.

Q: Television remote interview style (where the candidates are in a studio, seated, looking into cameras; the television audience would usually only see a talking-head framed shot of each participant, similar to ABC's Nightline *program, either full-screen or split-screen)?*

BROWN: These programs may be helpful in eliciting information, but candidates often seem less comfortable in this format, which audiences will sense. It doesn't necessarily make for a fluid conversation, as the interviewer and candidates may talk over one another inadvertently.

Q: When a candidate debate is held in a room other than a TV studio, what factors should be considered in terms of the type of facility that is needed?

BROWN: The most important one is whether the event can be handled with technical proficiency. Is the facility equipped for television production? If not, how are you going to turn it into a first-rate production facility and what will it cost? The sponsor needs to develop a budget early on so there are no surprises about what needs to be underwritten down the way. One way to control costs is to get venues and services donated free of charge. Access is an important issue.

116

Can people get to the facility easily even during rush hour? Are the police satisfied that the debate won't conflict with other events and vice versa? Can the facility be made secure in terms of candidate and journalist access? Those issues should be considered before you make a final decision on debate location.

Q: What about equipment requirements? What do debate sponsors need to know about that and if they don't know about it where can they get it?

BROWN: The most important thing is to consider television and radio broadcast needs and any other issues that address coverage of the debate. If sponsors have questions, they should consult experienced people familiar with those kinds of issues. Ask a local television station if they have any alumni who might be available to help.

Q: Are there ways to hold down costs without harming the quality of the program?

BROWN: The main thing is to do a budget first. What is absolutely necessary for the purpose of the debate? Then, what's on a wish list of things you'd like to do if you had the resources. Develop a budget and make sure it reflects everything that could reasonably be required. Try to figure out how you can raise those funds or how services might be donated, perhaps earning the donors recognition.

Q: Let's talk about audience control. When a live public audience is invited to attend a debate, what are the best ways to ensure the audience is balanced between supporters of the candidates? What is the best way to avoid audience disruptions, excessive applause, laughter, jeering and noise? Should the audience have to have tickets for entry? If so, where do they get them? Should they be free? How should tickets be allocated?

BROWN: The audience question is one of the stickiest

that we deal with. Obviously, when you have a debate there are a lot of members of the community who would like to attend. But it is extremely important not to have such a large audience that it poses built-in difficulties, such as noise or security problems. In presidential debates, the tickets are divided between the candidates who are debate participants and the commission. The commission's tickets go exclusively to the people who have helped produce the event, to donors, host site officials and community volunteers who have helped put it together.

It is inevitable that supporters of a candidate will want to make their feelings known. It puts the burden on both the sponsoring organization and the moderator to make it very clear up-front that audience noise is unfair to the candidates and unhelpful to the debate because, in a broadcast, it is unclear to viewers and listeners where the noise is coming from. Cameras are usually directed to only the participants on stage.

You have to persuade the audience that it is rude to take up time with intrusions. At the end of the day, disruptions and noise take away time from their candidates.

We have never sold tickets to presidential debates. The CPD is a non-profit, nonpartisan organization and selling tickets is not something that we have thought appropriate. The main thing is for the sponsor to allocate and distribute tickets in a fair manner that doesn't get in the way of putting on a useful event.

Q: Timekeeping is an important feature of most debates. What methods do you think work best? And which methods should be avoided? What signal devices should be used?

BROWN: Timekeeping is extremely important. You need someone whose job is solely timekeeping. Do not assign that task to the moderator. There are different ways to do this, but we have someone at the production table who is in charge of the clock.

The method that we have used to signal the candidates is

very simple. It's a series of traffic lights - green, amber and red – that are within the view of the candidates. They can be activated by the timekeeper so that it is clear to the candidates how much time they have left. The moderator has to enforce the time limits and be prepared to tell the candidates when they have run over.

Q: At what point should the candidates be signaled?

BROWN: In presidential debates, the green light goes on when their time starts. When they have 15 seconds to go, the amber light goes on. When their time is up, the red light goes on.

Q: You actually use an electronic device for this?

BROWN: It's very simple and inexpensive. Oversized cards can be used instead, but you want to make sure that the timekeeper is not trying to get the candidates' attention in a way that is distracting.

Q: When candidates and their campaigns negotiate debate rules and format features with sponsoring organizations, are there any issues that should be fixed and taken off the negotiating table?

BROWN: The sponsoring organization should make a recommendation for the debate that focuses on the important issues. In other words: the number of debates, the length of debates, the topics, single moderator or panel.

Put the big issues in a format recommendation and place it in front of the candidates as a starting point. Obviously, candidates will want a say, but it's the sponsor's duty to represent the interest of the public.

Simple is always better. Try to keep to the issues that affect the utility and the quality of the debate.

Q: What input should candidates and campaigns have in

debates once the basic rules are set and the format is decided?

BROWN: Candidates and campaigns have their own objectives in debate negotiations. Again, the main thing is for the debate sponsor to keep the interest of the public in mind. If the campaigns and the candidates have issues they feel strongly about, that's fine – put those on the table and try to reach a fair resolution. They may relate to rather specific details that have to do with the way candidates come onto the stage, the order of speaking and manner of introduction. There is no end to what candidates and campaigns may want to raise.

Q: What about candidates that want to renegotiate points after they were decided? Is there a way to stop that?

BROWN: The public needs to understand what the sponsor is recommending, and why the recommendation best serves their interests. If points come up for renegotiation as a campaign strategy, and they aren't serving the public interest, the sponsor should point this out.

Once decisions are made, I would strongly urge a sponsor to move on. You can renegotiate up to the eleventh hour, and that can start to affect your costs if you have to rework things. At the end of the day, you don't want surprises, budgetary or otherwise.

Q: How and when should sponsors invite candidates to participate?

BROWN: The earlier you contact campaigns, the less they can claim that they weren't kept informed, or that they scheduled something else and can't come. The more you can keep campaigns informed, the better chance you will have in bringing everybody together.

Q: Is there anything to know about the actual invitation? Does a letter suffice? A phone call? Should there be some docu-

mentation that everybody was invited on the same day? That there wasn't unfairness in the process?

BROWN: Sponsors should be business-like and absolutely fair, in order to show that no campaign is being favored or left behind. A letter of invitation to come to a meeting, or a letter outlining the sponsor's plans, is the best way of doing it. Again, the sponsor wants to be able to say to the public this is the way we proceeded and these are the responses we got.

Q: Do you think candidates should be allowed to use props and visuals?

BROWN: Once you open the door to props and visuals, it's hard to know where to draw the line. If someone arrives with large charts and pointers, where does it stop?

If you want to allow props and visuals, you must make sure the rules are fair to all the candidates. This is also a production question. If you have charts, you have to cue your camera people when to focus on them so that they will be legible to the home audience.

Whatever you do, get the ground rules straight from the start.

Q: What about notes? Should they be able to bring in papers, index cards and other documents? Where does it stop?

BROWN: A sponsor may decide notes are OK. But consider whether you want candidates rifling through papers and looking for documents while they are on the stage. The candidate may feel notes are helpful. Referring to them may not seem effective to the home audience, who may prefer to hear what the candidate says instead of watching him or her look for a citation.

Decide what you think will be helpful to the audience and make a recommendation to the candidates with an explanation for it.

Q: In terms of sponsoring debates for statewide candidates for, let's say, gubernatorial and U.S. Senate elections, what do you think is the minimum length the program should be? How about the maximum length?

BROWN: If you have a limit on the amount of time that a candidate can take to answer a question, divide that amount of time into the length of the debate and you'll discover how many questions you can ask and, therefore, how many topics you can cover. I don't think you can have a particularly effective debate for any major office in under 60 minutes. By the time you take out the introduction and either opening or closing statements, you don't have a great deal of time. If you go more than 90 minutes you are apt to lose some of your audience. The total number of debates factors in as well.

Q: What about when television producers want to fit a debate within the confines of a pre-existing television program? Is there any way to do that well? Perhaps limiting it to a single topic area?

BROWN: If you limit it to one topic, and you have an experienced interviewer who can conduct a focused conversation, that is the best way to try to do a debate within a 30-minute show. But again, if that's a half-hour commercial broadcast, and you have to take out time for ads, you are down to a small amount of time for actual discussion.

Q: What about downballot offices, such as the U.S. House, state legislative seats and local offices?

BROWN: Having debates is better than not having debates. If the only way to have one is to have a 30- or 45-minute discussion, then by all means do that. The time limit shouldn't be an obstacle. But, unless you firmly structure a conversation, 30 to 45 minutes can go by in a hurry – especially when you are addressing a broad range of topics.

Q: What considerations should go into deciding how long opening and closing statements should be?

BROWN: The public suspects that opening and closing statements are pre-rehearsed speeches. If you have closing statements, you don't necessarily need opening statements – particularly at the end of a rather long campaign. Quite often, closing statements reflect something about the debate that just preceded them. In either event, two minutes is enough. If it's any longer, it starts to be significant time taken away from the debate.

Q: What about answers to questions? How long should they be?

BROWN: Ours have always been 2 minutes. We have tried, as you know, to loosen debate rules so that the moderator didn't have to work with strict time limits and could basically serve as a traffic cop facilitating questions and answers back and forth. So far we have not been 100 percent successful in getting time limits taken off. Candidates are used to time limits and tend to like them.

Q: How about rebuttals and responses to rebuttals?

BROWN: Our rebuttals are limited to 1 minute. We don't have responses to rebuttals, mainly to keep things moving so the candidates can address more topics.

Q: What is the best, fairest way to select a debate moderator?

BROWN: We look for three attributes: (1) someone who is familiar with the candidates and the important campaign issues, (2) someone who has had extensive television experience and will be able to handle the technical responsibilities, and (3) someone who will remember that their name is not on the ballot and that they are not on stage to compete with the candidates but to facilitate a conversation. It is extremely important that the method of selecting a moderator be handled discreetly, fairly and efficiently. Names should not be tossed out, publicly, for consideration. The selection process should also be handled in a way that gives the moderator ample time to prepare.

Q: How about debate questioners, if there are questioners in addition to a moderator?

BROWN: Again, the same three attributes that go into the selection of the moderator are equally important for debate questioners. Panelists should be discouraged from asking the "gotcha" question, which may showcase the panelist's area of expertise but not produce a particularly informative response. Clearly, if you are going to have several questioners, you should be aware of representation on the panel. If it's going to be a panel of journalists, you want to make sure you have both print and electronic journalists that represent different segments of the market. The most important thing is that they take their responsibilities very seriously – which is to get information from the candidates that's helpful to the viewers and listeners.

Q: What input should the candidates have in the selection of questioners?

BROWN: Input from any source, if provided respectfully and discreetly, is helpful. The debate sponsor needs names of people for the panel who are respected and responsible, and who will take this duty very seriously. Questioner selection should not be a protracted public process.

Q: How should debate moderators prepare themselves?

BROWN: The first task is to be familiar with the issues that are of the greatest interest to the public. Moderators also need to understand how to ask questions that will get new information on the record for the benefit of the people who are watching, listening to and reading about the debate. They also need experience in the technical aspects of the debate.

Q: How tough should moderators be in enforcing rules? When is flexibility allowable and where?

BROWN: The moderator needs to be someone who is going to be comfortable in the debate, which is a high stakes event, and also in interrupting if need be, which is difficult. It can be intimidating, but the moderator must keep the debate on track and fair. By the same token, let's assume that the debate is going along so well that a serious, substantive discussion has taken off. If that means the moderator needs to give a little more time to let the candidates keep going with it, personally I think that is a good idea. But it takes a lot of discretion and self-confidence on the part of the moderator.

Q: What if a candidate repeatedly violates rules – let's say interrupting his or her opponent or refusing to abide by time limits? How should the moderator handle it?

BROWN: Moderators in presidential debates are prepared to say, "Excuse me, candidates, but if you do not stick by the rules as you accepted them, we will stop the program and renegotiate the rules." They are prepared to point out that the sponsoring organization came up with the format and tell the candidates, "You agreed to it and you are not sticking by it. If you want to change the rules that's fine but we are not going to make it up as we go along." That can involve a little bit of tension, but it may need to be said. It's not fair to other candidates to have one candidate change the rules on the spot. A moderator needs to figure out ahead of time how control will be maintained.

Q: In taking those experiences and applying them to state and local elections, downballot candidates may be willing to take chances that presidential candidates are unwilling to take. What is the ultimate sanction for a candidate who just isn't behaving properly? Is it stopping the debate? Is it asking the candidate to leave the debate? Is it turning off the candidate's microphone?

BROWN: Any of those are options, if need be. The sponsor and the moderator need to decide up-front if something gets out of hand what they are going to do about it. The same question applies if someone in the audience gets out of hand. You need to decide how are you going to address a situation that goes differently than planned. That way you won't leave the moderator out there trying to wing it.

Q: When there are audience questions for the candidates, what is the best way to select the members of the audience who will ask the questions? What about screening the questions? What methods work best?

BROWN: When we have had town meeting debates, the Gallup Organization has selected the participants. Their threshold question for participants chosen by telephone interviews was whether they had decided for whom to vote. Our objective was to get undecided voters. You clearly want to avoid having an audience that is skewed for one candidate or one party. There are lots of different ways to achieve balance, but make sure you do.

In our 2000 town meeting, audience members were asked to submit two or three questions several hours beforehand to ensure a representative range of topics. The moderator can then select the questions to be asked and call on the individuals who submitted them to actually pose the questions to the candidates.

Q: Should the candidates have access to staff members during debates?

BROWN: That is not a good idea. Once you start the debate, allowing other people to come on stage – absent some health emergency or production problem – isn't very helpful to the audience that is trying to focus on the candidates.

Q: How do you ensure that a TV production crew shows fairness to the candidates participating, on issues such as reaction shots, shot framing, sound quality and lighting?

BROWN: It is very important that the production crew understand that the sponsor is responsible for the event and that the sponsor needs to be absolutely fair. The audience is not going to be well-served if the debate is less than optimal on any front, whether it is lighting, sound, the set or anything else.

With regard to reaction shots, shot framing, things like that, we have an understanding up-front of what will be allowed and what will not. Decide how many cameras will be used, where will they be placed and what they will cover. That way, candidates can't say, "I didn't understand that this would be allowed and I think it was unfair."

Q: What about candidate make-up? Microphones? Allowances for physical limitations?

BROWN: Candidates should be responsible for their own make-up. The debate sponsors should be responsible for microphones and the sound system. We use fixed microphones, no hand-held ones. Our microphones all have back-up systems.

Obviously the sponsor should ensure that the set allows for any candidate's physical limitations to be accommodated in a way that is fair and dignified.

Q: Any tips for set design? Furniture? Platforms? Backdrops? Chair and stools?

BROWN: Simple is always better. Sets should be handsome but plain. The dark royal blue backdrop that presidential debates have used is very complimentary. The furniture should be unmarked and comfortable. Stay away from busy and cluttered.

The crew that designs and builds the set for the presidential debates does sets for television stations all over the country. These kinds of professionals are available through the Presidential Debate Commission to help local sponsors decide on the look that they want and how to achieve it at a reasonable cost.

Q: What kind of staff is needed to manage a debate held at a public facility?

BROWN: You don't need a large staff, but you do need some experienced people to make sure things go smoothly. Someone needs to be responsible for all the different things we've covered, including where the media will be accommodated and have access to candidates afterwards. There is plenty of room for volunteers. But you don't want to put a volunteer in charge of something that they have had no experience with. This is a great time to look for people in your community who have experience with political and media events and ask if they could give some time and expertise.

Q: Are there any legal issues a debate sponsor should know about? Including FCC, FEC and IRS rules? Copyright and rebroadcast rights?

BROWN: That is a really important issue, I'm glad you raised it. Any debate sponsor should thoroughly research all federal, state or local rules that might apply to the broadcast, to the debate itself, to the rebroadcast, to the transcript and to who is invited to participate in the debate. Research those issues ahead of time. If it means touching base early with an attorney with broadcast or election law expertise, do it.

Getting information up-front helps avoid problems on the back end.

Q: What should media organizations do to promote debates to ensure there is a large audience?

BROWN: Debates are about civic education. In our experience, the more attention is focused on the debates the more opportunity there is for the public to learn from the debates. Media organizations should not only promote the debate itself but also take advantage of the opportunity to publish articles, sponsor pre-debate forums and distribute other materials that give helpful information for the public to review ahead of time. Our Debate Watch program was created to evaluate the debates and find out whether people found them helpful. Initiatives like this can help increase a debate's effectiveness as an educational event and give the debate sponsor more bang for the buck.

Q: If a debate sponsor wants to encourage more substantive discussion of serious issues in a debate, and discourage prepackaged sound bites and empty sloganeering, are there any tips you'd recommend in terms of the format and the rules?

BROWN: The looser the rules the better. Have a seasoned moderator. Don't allow materials or props in the debate. These steps should maximize your chances of having the candidates answer questions in a way that isn't prepackaged and that hopefully will spark a substantive conversation. The more predictable the questions and the less spontaneous the conversation, the more you will hear the same prepackaged answer that you've heard before.

Q: So it really requires a lot of trust in the moderator?

BROWN: A lot of trust. The moderator must be familiar with the candidates and issues so that he or she can bring out new information that voters may not have heard before during the campaign.

Q: What services does the Presidential Debate Commission offer to media and civic organizations who want to sponsor non-presidential debates?

BROWN: We are here to help in anyway we can on two fronts. One is production. If we can help a sponsor understand anything that has to do with format or negotiation or promotion or technical issues, we are delighted to do that. The second is on the voter education front. We have tried different programs ever since our first debates in `88 and many can be adapted to other races.

If debate sponsors call or e-mail the Commission, I am happy to talk with them. If they have a specific question that needs input from our production crew, I'm delighted to refer them to those individuals.

Q: What are the most often asked questions you get from state and local debate sponsors and media people?

BROWN: The most often asked questions relate to how the sponsor plans the debate on three fronts: (1) How do you negotiate with candidates? (2) What's the best way to develop a sound format? and (3) How do you put the event together? We have had a lot of experience in all three areas so we can often save people headaches – and are delighted to do so.

CHAPTER 9

Voices of Experience: What Debate Organizers Have Learned

By David Beiler

In an effort to learn from the recent experiences of those who have sponsored campaign debates, and to share in the wisdom of their advice, we interviewed a dozen debate organizers from a variety of organizations. Between them, those interviewed have helped administer over a hundred debates covering all levels of the ballot.

The following profiles of these organizers relate the context and particulars of their individual experiences, along with innovations they have pioneered or suggest be tried in the future. There follows a point-by-point analysis of common debate components that utilizes these organizers as an advisory board, offering consensus opinions on some issues and controversies on others, with illustrative comments on each.

The reader will quickly discern a dichotomy emerging from the widely varying case studies and sage advice: High-profile races for high-powered offices generate debates that are commonly carried by major television outlets, a fact that professionalizes the event and largely dictates its particulars. Debates in races for lesser office tend to involve the public more directly, and often bear some imprint of the hosting organization's particular interests and agenda.

Sue Adams
Smart Growth Director

Pilchuk Audubon Club
Everett, Wash.

Acting often in concert with other environmental groups, the League of Women Voters and occasionally non-profits with dissimilar interest, Pilchuk has hosted debates at all levels in recent years, except the U.S. House. Although none have been broadcast live, some have been taped for later broadcast on cable TV, and news coverage has been forthcoming from all types of media. Venues for these events have ranged widely: large theaters for the high-profile, statewide contests; small Grange halls for local, rural races.

As the member in charge of Pilchuk's most explosive political front, Adams has been in the forefront of planning the Club's debate sponsorships. Her objectives are to raise the profile of the Club's issues in the public discourse, get candidates to commit on them, and inform the public of these stands. In theory, this will result in public policies in line with the group's goals.

Pilchuk debates are conducted by a moderator from a well-known organization – usually the LWV. Questions are taken from the audience on 3x5 cards and reviewed by a screener from the sponsor before being passed on to the moderator. The screener will gang questions of a similar type, edit for length and clarity, and cull out those which appear to be diatribes for a particular point of view, seem loaded against a particular candidate or are just plain "kooky," Adams explains. "We sometimes get these things from folks who have seen black helicopters streaming in over the Canadian border."

As an organization devoted to a particular set of causes, Pilchuk is loath to use formats that would lessen their control over the debates. The only points they are willing to negotiate with campaigns are the length and date of the debate. As "professional" panelists (journalists, professors, etc.) would not stand for the screening of their questions, the Club avoids using them. Much the same reason is given for not allowing candidates to question each other, though Adams admits it could invigorate the proceedings and might be tried in the future "under certain constraints," such as no attacks and no follow-ups.

The Club is adamant about inviting all candidates to participate and opening the audience to all who wish to attend. That conviction may be responsible for the fact that Pilchuk's debates have not been broadcast live or shown on a delayed basis by major television outlets, which often balk at venues outside their own studios because of added costs.

Greg Borum
Executive Director
The Citizen's Project
Boulder, Colo.

The Citizen's Project came into being a decade ago, when Christian conservative candidates began to win large numbers of local elected offices in Colorado, particularly on school boards. Such groups as the Christian Coalition and Focus on the Family were inspiring and advising such campaigns, and using grassroots organizing to commandeer party caucuses and low-turnout elections.

Alarmed at the sudden swing in public policies toward fundamentalist doctrine, several groups devoted to separation of church and state organized The Citizen's Project to inform voters of candidate intentions. At the center of this mission has been sponsoring debates, usually in conjunction with media outlets. Other co-sponsors have included the LWV, the NAACP, the Interfaith Alliance and the Urban League. These groups provide volunteers for the event and help publicize it.

The Project's debates usually run 90 minutes and have thus far been limited to elections for local office and the state legislature. They are often taped and broadcast on public access television, and frequently attract coverage in local newspapers and the newscasts of commercial TV stations.

Moderators are usually members of the news media, since that way "you're guaranteed coverage by at least one outlet," Borum observes. All questions are taken in written form from the audience and are screened by members of the LWV, due to their reputation for objectivity. Borum likes the idea of allowing candidates to question each other and promises to experiment with the format in the future. "I think it would make it livelier and more interesting," he speculates.

Project debates often have candidates from several races onstage at once, if they are running for seats on the same body. "That's unfortunate," Borum concedes. "People then have to listen to people they can't vote for while waiting for those candidates who will be on their ballots." The device is largely a matter of logistical necessity, but "we also believe people should be educated about candidates outside their area, as they will still impact your area" if elected.

Borum is willing to negotiate the date and physical format of a debate, as well as some stage details, but holds firm on other points. His limited flexibility has raised the hackles of at least one candidate, who bitterly protested a rule against setting up campaign tables and posting signs by the entrance to the hall. "He had cleared a church table of Sunday school literature and claimed it for his campaign headquarters for the night," Borum recalls. Volunteers restored the table and cleared posted signs after the candidate's campaign refused.

Rick Brush
President and CEO
California Society of Association Executives (CAL-SAE)

Brush's group is unusual in that it specializes in hosting debates about ballot questions – those exercises in direct democracy that play such an important role in governing our largest state. Over the past years, CAL-SAE events have explored the pros and cons of four proposals before the voters, zeroing in on issues that were likely to affect the highest percentage of its members.

What led the Society into this unusual niche?

"We wanted to inform our people about issues that could very well impact what they do," explains Brush. "It all started with one of our board members, who is an active lobbyist and was involved in one of the [2000] campaigns. He suggested it, and we thought it would be a good forum for our members to meet and learn from some heavy-hitters in the legislature."

To help defray expenses and help promotion, the Society arranged co-sponsorships with the California Chamber of Commerce and the Voter Education Committee of the California Labor Federation. The debates were moderated by Jack Cavanaugh – a veteran political reporter who now edits a political newsletter. Questions were fielded from the audience, which was opened to anyone willing to pay the $55 registration fee. Participants were also given the opportunity to question each other.

"That stirred up a little controversy . . . [and] kept the listeners interested," Brush reports. "It was the best part."

Most of the debaters were legislators. "We always try to get the sponsors of the bill, if it is a referendum," reveals Brush, who will also try to find advocates and opponents of an initiative among the ranks of the State Assembly. The Society's debates are, after all, pitched mainly to lobbyists as meet-and-greets with Capitol bigwigs.

The targeted audience is largely responsible for the choice of venue – a hotel ballroom within walking distance of the Capitol and the Society's offices. But Brush's initial choice of facilities caused consternation among some of the participants: "We originally scheduled for a non-union hotel," he recalls. "The Democrats declared they wouldn't come because of that, so we scratched . . . [and] found a union hotel."

Brush was not open to other alterations, other than the time of the event.

A public relations firm was hired to publicize the debates, and the Society's pivotal position as an umbrella organization for association execs was a boon to promotion: "We put out a notice of the meeting to our members," Brush details, "so they could include it in communications with their members."

The results were gratifying, with coverage from commercial television, three radio stations and several newspapers.

But the Society may be ready to abandon its new role. After losing less than $1,000 on its 2000 forum, the CAL-SAE's effort in 2002 was a disaster. With the debate only two weeks away, pre-registrations could be counted on one hand and the event was canceled.

Brush is philosophical about the reverse. "Maybe we'll go back to having them in conjunction with luncheons," he speculates.

Carolyn Chase
Former President
Sierra Club of San Diego County, Calif.

In California, organizations like the Sierra Club (the state's largest environmental group) tend to look upon their candidate debates as job interviews. They are often conducted very early: July being a common debate date, largely because the deadline for getting your name on the ballot alongside those of your favorite candidates is in August.

That's right: California allows candidates to list endorsers on the ballot with them.

The process has led partisan groups to host campaign debates as a means of gathering information they can use in reckoning their endorsement. It also "lets us get the candidates on record," notes Chase, who suggests assurances made in private may not be the coin of the realm.

"We also want to generate publicity for the endorsement," she elaborates, "which often comes shortly after the debate. And it helps us build coalitions with groups of similar interests."

Indeed, 15 different organizations each got to pose a question to the candidates for San Diego mayor at the Club's 2000 forum. The candidates are never bewildered by this array of interviewers; however, they get to see all the questions in advance.

"We want to give them a chance to come up with the right answer," explains the generous Chase, who even offers to help the candidates with their homework. If they tell club members what they want to hear, so much the better. The

Sierrans have it on videotape and will hold them to their word.

The Sierra Club's San Diego chapter has thus far limited its debates to local races. They are typically taped for later broadcast on cable TV and sometimes attract print media attention, particularly when the mayoralty is at stake. "It has to be off-beat or a slow news day for them to cover anything else," sighs Chase.

University settings are the favorite venue, but library rooms, churches and union halls have also been pressed into service. "Whatever we can get for free," Chase explains. "I moderate, because it is our event and we want to maintain control." There is no panel, per se, but pre-arranged questions are presented by representatives of the other organizations taking part. (These are not formal co-sponsors since "we keep expenses down and don't need them to defray the costs.") Questions from the audience are screened, with dupes weeded out and phraseology condensed.

The tight control Chase and the club maintain over their events extends to dealings with the candidates, where only the date, audience composition and a few physical format issues are allowed on the table. Third party and minor candidates are often excluded, a process the Sierran admits is "political."

Despite running a tight ship, Chase would like to see debates that are more of a free-for-all:

"The League of Women Voters screens out all the interesting stuff. They want to make things as boring as possible . . . An open, back-and-forth format can be fascinating, but you've got to have a great moderator and make sure the candidates understand the rules, or it can be a disaster."

Gino DeCaro
California Association of Manufacturers (CAM)
Sacramento, Calif.

In 1998 CAM co-sponsored a debate for the California gubernatorial race, at the request of the California Labor Federation. (The unions were seeking a counter-balance to their own sponsorship to assure candidates and the public that the event would be conducted without bias.) The Federation again approached CAM about sponsoring a debate in 2002, but the manufacturers decided they could not afford the expense at this time.

CAM does not rule out debate sponsorship in the future, however, if the funds are there and the advantages are as apparent as they were in 1998: "We saw [then-Lt. Gov. Gray] Davis [a Democrat] as the likely winner," reveals DeCaro, "and wanted to demonstrate our willingness to work with him and labor to make California a better state in which to do business."

Because of the high profile of the race, the debate attracted a horde of media attention with little effort. It was held in the San Diego convention center, and was broadcast live on local television.

The co-sponsors selected the moderator and panelists without input from the campaigns and looked for a balance of ideologies and interests. Questions were not screened or restricted because "if you are careful with your questioner selection, you don't have to worry about inappropriate questions."

Questions from the large audience were not taken as "it would have opened up a lot of issues about structure," De Caro explains, "[and] we didn't have time to deal with that." He believes audience questions have their place in untelevised debates for lower office, which do not have to deal with as many constraints, such as the requirements of television stations.

Such requirements and the desire to concentrate on the concerns of their members caused the co-sponsors to take a fairly stiff stance in negotiations with the campaigns. Only the debate's date, length and physical format were open to adjustment.

Larry Freundlich
Debate Coordinator
American Jewish Committee, central N. J. chapters

AJC has hosted debates in races at all levels, except governor, working in conjunction with several Jewish groups.

"We like to have access and influence policy," says Freundlich. "By taking an active role in providing candidates access to our community, there is a quid pro quo of having our opinions heard when these people take office."

AJC debates have been broadcast on cable television and been covered by commercial TV stations, radio and print – including *The New York Times*. The venue has almost always been a temple.

"We have been offered TV studios," Freundlich reveals, "but have declined. An organization like ours is interested in cultivating greater participation and membership, so we like to make it a public event."

In the past, receptions have generally been held before the event, but without the candidates present. Freundlich thinks AJC may soon experiment with having the receptions subsequent to the debates, with the candidates on hand to meet, greet and answer follow-ups in a sort of festive press-op/postgame show. "We are a social organization as well as a service organization," he reminds.

AJC's formatting is a bit unusual, with a single lectern in the middle being used by both candidates, who sit on either side. A moderator and three panelists ask the questions; queries were fielded from the audience in the past, but are now avoided. "It was too cumbersome, on-the-spot," complains Freundlich, who has served as moderator. "Here I was, expected to keep track of the candidates and conduct the debate, and juggle these questions, too." He is receptive to the idea of having someone other than the moderator screen audience questions, however, and may try to arrange future debates in such a fashion.

Consequently, Freundlich's recommended debate format departs from what he uses in that he would now include a segment driven by questions from the audience. It would follow a panelist questioning segment of similar duration in a 60-minute event format, bookended by brief opening and closing statements.

In terms of negotiating with the candidates, AJC was the most pliant of all organizations surveyed. Only the length of the debate, audience composition, and length of questions and responses are completely off the table, as is question screening – unless a ban on personal questions is requested.

Roy Miller, Chairman
Jason Zaborski, Executive Director
Florida Children's Campaign (FCC)
Tallahassee, Fla.

Operating on the theory that teenagers can best advance their issues through public interrogation of political candidates, the Children's Campaign has had a significant impact in a very brief period of time. In just four years it has taken the lead in organizing 15 debates for various offices across the state, produced a "how-to" handbook for debate organizers, released a promotional video and opened a branch office in Kansas. Its innovative events have generated a considerable amount of media attention and have been credited with providing pivotal moments for some races.

It all began with a 1998 debate between the candidates for state education commissioner. The contestants were questioned by high school students from across the state in what proved to be their only direct confrontation prior to the general election. The hourlong forum was shown live on public television stations across Florida.

Student participants were nominated by county school superintendents, education foundations and selected community agencies. These sponsors paid for the students' expenses and provided chaperones. Subsequent events have generally followed this intriguing format, designed to get youth involved in state and local politics.

Affiliated with the Florida Center for Children and Youth and the Coalition for America's Children, FCC is the brainchild of Miller, a professional political consultant with 65 campaigns to his credit.

"While serving those clients, I was amazed at the lack of substantive scrutiny they received at campaign forums,"

Miller explains. "I found myself saying, 'I bet kids will ask better questions. They'll do the research.' Debate panelists from various groups didn't want to ruffle feathers, didn't want to alienate the incumbent. Kids don't have those constrictions."

In an FCC debate for a state Senate seat, the well-heeled frontrunner dissolved into stammering incoherence after a young girl asked for his position on sex education. His campaign soon dissolved with him.

When a high schooler asked an incumbent legislator for her position on desalination, she gave a tentative, confused answer, admitting the issue wasn't on her "front burner of environmental issues." Noting that the legislator had touted herself as an environmentalist, the student asked what was on that front burner.

"[The legislator] took a full two steps back from the microphone and waited for what seemed an eternity to answer," Miller recalls. A favorite going into the debate, the candidate lost.

But Miller's motivations go beyond seeing the candidates get a hard look from the electorate: "We want a true discussion of children's issues between the candidates, not their prepackaged slogans and sound bites. We want to promote youth empowerment."

FCC's biggest hurdle has been to show the news media that it produces serious events, not a cute kids' show. It is a problem that is beginning to fade.

"Now we have a track record we can show people," Miller points out. "We send out video and newspaper clips that show we've had an impact."

FCC begins its process by contacting schools and youth service organizations within the constituency of a targeted office; concurring institutions are then sent applications that refer to 35-40 topics of public policy. Returned applications are reviewed by the FCC staff and invitations are extended, carefully balanced for geography, gender and race.

"The students do their own research, write their questions and submit them to us," Miller recounts. "We edit for length and clarity and make sure it applies to the office." The moderator is always a newsperson "of stature and the proper background."

FCC solicits co-sponsors and usually has five or six for each debate. In the past, these have included the League of Women Voters, the United Way, the YMCA and corporations interested in children's issues. Local coordinators are lined up early in the process and required to sign an agreement. A co-sponsorship slot is reserved for the television outlet, if one is carrying the event. Such media sponsorship has already run the full gamut, with affiliates of all four major broadcast networks, local public stations and the PBS statewide network having all filled the niche at one time or another.

When debates are broadcast on live TV, the venue is usually the studio of the co-sponsoring station. Those for lower profile races are usually held in auditorium or gyms, but never in a facility with a religious affiliation.

In yet another innovation, Children's Campaign debates sometimes feature an "open minute" at the event's midpoint, where candidates have 60 seconds to clarify a point of their choice.

Stacey Patricoski
Executive Director
League of Women Voters of Illinois

A large and diverse state, Illinois provides a representative microcosm for the experiences of that most seasoned debate sponsor, the League of Women Voters. The state office handles debates for several statewide elections, while 50 local chapters cover the downballot at all levels.

"Our historical mission has been to get information about issues and candidates out to the voters," relates Patricoski. "This is our 33rd year of [hosting debates]. It's a good example of how we can carry out this mission."

The League's statewide events are often very high-profile, with as many as 30 media representatives on hand. They watch the debate in a "green room," where candidates are later brought in for 10 minutes at a time for post-game press opportunities. "We try to get maximum exposure to the broadest possible audience," Patricoski explains.

The host TV stations usually tape the program for later use, but occasionally broadcast live, and even put the event on satellite so other outlets can downlink excerpts for their evening newscasts. One downside to this seeming generosity is the fact these stations invariably insist on selecting the moderator – and usually choose their lead anchor.

"NBC and CBS aren't going to promote a debate sponsored by ABC and conducted by ABC's own talent," laments Patricoski, who also suggests a conflict of interest may lead these moderators to hyperactivity: "There is no way a TV personality is going to give up an opportunity for more face time."

Another drawback to the TV partnerships is the reluctance of the stations to venture beyond their own studios, leading to the absence of a substantial live audience. In the 1980s, the Illinois League's gubernatorial and U.S. Senate debates were often staged in large Chicago halls, and electronically connected to still more live audiences downstate via remote feed. Today, the stations and the League cannot afford the great expense required by such staging.

True to their TV broadcast constraints, League statewide debates today usually run 60 minutes. Panels consist of four journalists, with a preference for reporters over columnists, due to their perceived objectivity. Panel questions follow the opening remarks and precede the closings, but are sometimes (usually in primary debates) interrupted by a segment that allows the candidates to question one another. It is a practice Patricoski would like to see expanded: "Nobody knows better than the candidates themselves what the differences are between them."

Local League debates depart markedly from those run out of the state office. The events are usually televised, but typically by cable channels on a delayed basis. Auditoriums are the most popular venue, the time frame often runs 90 minutes or more, and candidates are more likely to sit at banquet tables facing the audience than stand behind podiums – particularly when three or more are involved. The moderator is a League member, and – if organizers follow the guidance of the state office – a political expert hailing from another constituency. Panelists are typically eschewed in favor of screened questions from the audience.

The state office will co-sponsor with the hosting TV station or the Illinois Association of Broadcasters, but rarely anyone else. Patricowski defends this seeming territorialism, contending, "There is a strong sense we have a market niche and an identity that is linked to debates . . . . We tend to not want to share the marquis."

By contrast, local Leagues are quick to welcome co-sponsors, such as colleges, newspapers and civic organizations. "It's a good way to forge partnerships . . . pool resources and leverage the number of volunteers," Patricoski advises. "There is a lot of work involved."

On the state League's table for negotiation with the candidates are the physical format, length of answers and statements, and stage details. When panelists are used, they are nominated by the League, but can be vetoed by a candidate.

But while the League is willing to negotiate with candidates, it will do so only in dead earnest: "We tell them to send someone who is in authority to make decisions for the campaign," declares Patricoski. "We will not leave that room until the rules are finalized."

One 1998 gubernatorial candidate backpedaled after the rules had been sent out, insisting his representative had not been empowered to make the decision after all. "I got the managers on a three-way conference call and made them settle it," Patricoski disdainfully recalls.

Terry Payne
President
National Association for the Advancement of Colored People (NAACP) – Stafford County, Va., Chapter
Payne's group got involved in debates because it saw a void – and an opportunity.

"We want to make the NAACP not just an advocacy group for civil rights issues, but also a group concerned with community-based issues, issues that impact the concerns of the broader community," he explains. "We see the value of the bully pulpit of campaigns to raise these issues. We haven't seen other organizations [hosting debates], so there was a void to fill. We also want to get people engaged, get them involved in politics, get them to register and vote."

So the Stafford chapter hosted debates between candidates for the state legislature, county board of supervisors and school board last year – eight races, all on a single night. (One candidate declined to take part, but his opponent was permitted to appear and 'debate' alone.)

"It was tough," Payne recalls. "People had to sit and listen to people they couldn't vote for. But a supervisor in another part of the county will have as much impact on your future as the supervisor from your district, so we felt the audience got something out of hearing all the candidates, not just the ones in their district." Still, he admits the combo format "got pretty unwieldy," and the event may be broken into two nights next time.

Payne sought no co-sponsors for the event, but has since had offers from organizations willing to team up in the future. He is open to forging such partnerships, but only if the other groups are as resolutely nonpartisan as his own.

The first NAACP debates in Stafford were held in 1999, in a small church that was packed to capacity. Two years later, the school system lent the group a high school auditorium.

"We really didn't need that much room," Payne admits, "but we wanted to be open to anyone. That was one reason we moved the site. The new site in the high school dramatized the fact the forum was open to everybody."

The 2001 debates attracted about 50 spectators, including reporters from two newspapers – a daily and a weekly. Index cards for writing questions were given to voters as they entered the hall. As moderator, Payne screened and presented the audience questions, as well as a couple of his own.

"One lesson we had to learn: Mix up the order in which the candidates answer questions, Payne relates. "The incumbent delegate protested that he was always answering first, which gave his opponent a consistent advantage in that she was able to rebut and he was not. So we mixed up the order from there on."

Despite the light turnout, Payne is satisfied with the debate project.

"We got great press – front page coverage. It proved to be an excellent opportunity for us to show our involvement in the community."

Nancy Reed
Fairfax County, Va., Chamber of Commerce (FCCC)

Among surveyed organizations, FCCC looks upon its sponsorship of debates as a revenue generator. That perceived role has largely driven the evolution of the group's debate practices.

"We used to host debates for county supervisor and the General Assembly," recounts Reed, "but those races don't draw sufficiently anymore. The stature of our debates has grown . . . . We now have little trouble getting all the candidates for federal and statewide office" and those events "generate far greater income."

One reason for FCCC's lofty stature is the key strategic nature of its constituency. A suburb of Washington, D.C., Fairfax has nearly a million residents, with a per capita income unsurpassed by any county in America of substantial size. The Chamber's debates are carried on Washington television stations, which is a very large and enormously expensive media market, with many of its viewers residing outside Virginia.

Reed's biggest headache is finding a hotel ballroom big enough to accommodate the 750 luncheoneers who register for her typical debate. These events are always combined with lunch because "it's a time people are not expecting to be scheduled," Reed explains. "The impact on the business day is not great."

But even taking in a debate over lunch has its time constraints.

"The time span people can commit is no more than 100 minutes," Reed details, "and you don't want to have the candidates talking while people are being served or dishes are being cleared. That leaves you about 50-55 minutes for the debate," which just happens to coincide with the perfect time block for TV stations, which want a few minutes of airtime to set the debate up in the minds of the viewers.

FCCC debates are routinely carried live by commercial channels, although last year was an exception. Held 17 days after the September 11 attacks, the gubernatorial scrap between Mark Warner (D) and Mark Earley (R) broke hibernations for both campaigns, and found television stations unwilling to commit large blocs of time to coverage unrelated to the terrorist threat. Under normal circumstances, the events are covered by dozens of journalists from TV, radio and print – a level of success Reed partly attributes to a gung-ho Chamber press officer with a "fantastic contact list."

Although Chamber debates are open to anyone willing to pay the registration fee, Reed concedes 90 percent of attendees are business people, a fact that influences the subjects pursued by the panel – three journalists and a representative from the local business community. No questions from the audience are entertained because "we're a big advocacy organization" that wants to keep questions on target, Reed explains.

For moderating, Reed looks for a well-known media person not ideologically identified in the public mind. In 2000 – FCCC's last debate under normal circumstances – that trail led to Tim Russert, host of NBC's *Meet the Press*.

Running an operation so powerful it actually turns a substantial profit, Reed can bargain with campaigns from a position of strength she is not shy to use. Apart from discussing the date and a few points of stagecraft, campaign managers can pretty well save their breath with her – and should consider themselves lucky.

"You think kindergartners are bad?" she moans. "Dealing with campaigns can be almost ludicrous."

The high profile of the Chamber debates and the control Reed exerts over them have occasionally spurred controversy. Third-party candidates are not invited, and Reed's exclusion of the Libertarian candidate for governor last year unleashed "hundreds and hundreds" of protesting e-mails from as far away as Seoul, South Korea. And when a campaign violated a Chamber rule against using debate footage for campaign purposes, threat of legal action brought belated compliance.

Ignorance of the rules is never a credible defense, as FCCC requires candidates to sign off on them in advance.

Carol Scott
National Board Member, League of Women Voters
Former President, League of Women Voters of Oklahoma

In Oklahoma – as in most states – the state League coordinates debates in statewide and some congressional races, while the local chapters run some in congressional races and everything further down the ballot. Scott says the League has such a vaunted reputation for debate sponsoring, candidates are often asking it to host debates before being asked to participate in one.

"Of course, we would do it on our own even if we weren't asked," she insists. "It's what the League is about. We've been doing it for decades."

The Oklahoma state League has its act down pat: It always co-sponsors debates with a TV outlet -- usually a commercial station in one of the two markets that virtually cover the state between them: Oklahoma City and Tulsa. That station will put the broadcast on feed to another station in the other market, creating what amounts to a statewide hookup. All such debates are staged in studios, where questions are asked only by panelists.

This pattern got a different wrinkle for a recent debate co-sponsored with the University of Oklahoma's Kanter

Archive of Political Advertising: The event was staged in a campus auditorium and carried on the state's public television network, a third co-sponsor.

With the exception of the rare university-based outfit, the Oklahoma state League avoids partnering with anyone other than a television host. "A lot of organizations – including chambers of commerce – want to focus debates on issues primary to their membership," Scott explains. "The League wants to cover all the issues the general public is interested in."

She acknowledges, however, that local League debates are often co-sponsored by such groups as a means of sharing expenses and – most importantly – getting the word out. It is a practice she actually encourages: "Local Leagues should take on more co-sponsors. That way, you can get more people out to the debate. You have to do anything you can to get information about the debate out. If it is not going to be televised, be sure to get the print media there. If only 20 people show and it isn't covered, you really haven't accomplished your mission."

How can news organizations be drawn to an event? "The media love sensationalism, and will show up if they expect to find controversy," Scott observes, falling short of any recommendation of professional-wrestling-style promotion. "Fortunately, we have no trouble attracting news coverage of our debates for statewide races."

State League formats invariably have the candidates behind podiums and the panel of questioners seated at a table. Local Leagues usually put the candidates behind a table as well, given the usual paucity of podiums and microphones at venues such as schools and community centers. Constrained by the realities of broadcast television schedules, statewide debates run 45-55 minutes. That is fine with Scott, who contends "more than 60 minutes is exhausting for everyone." She acknowledges, however, that local debates can (and often do) run longer. In fact they should, she admits, if a large number of candidates are involved.

Because Scott likes things to run smoothly, she prefers the

tight control of a TV studio with little or no audience, and would even have the moderator ask all the questions "in a perfect world." In practice, she admits, such a task may be beyond the moderator's capabilities.

The problem is hosting stations push their anchors for the job, she complains. "One had an anchor known as a pretty face, and they wanted him to gain more credibility. He tried to push the opportunity by doing more than a moderator really ought to. He started giving his opinions . . . . It was really inappropriate."

Apart from the date of the debate, the state League does not negotiate particulars with campaigns. Rather, it sends its proposed rules and format to them and considers suggested changes, most liberally with regard to physical format and statement/question length. Candidates must sign their agreement to the final configuration.

The biggest debate dispute Oklahoma's League has had to weather in recent years was ignited by its refusal to invite the gubernatorial nominee of the Reform Party – then one of only three parties legally recognized by the state.

"We took a lot of flak for that," recalls Scott. "Because they were a recognized party, I had a bit of a problem with that myself . . . . I think we might change the criteria for third party candidates in the future."

Russell Verney
Executive Director – New Hampshire Democratic Party (1986-92)
Issues Director – United We Stand, America (1993-94)
Currently: Judicial Watch – Dallas, Texas

Verney helped stage candidate debates while coordinating Democrats in New Hampshire, including those between contestants in that state's ballyhooed presidential primary. Later, while guiding Ross Perot's citizens organization, he staged a series of debates between candidates in a special U.S. Senate election. Those events served as a pilot project for scores of United We Stand-sponsored candidate debates across the country in 1994, which Verney advised.

Verney's debates were generally carried live on commercial TV and radio outlets and received extensive coverage in all media forms then in widespread use. He credits his publicity success to three factors: 1) scheduling the debate close to the election, after the media frenzy has moved into full gear; 2) urging the campaigns to work their own media contacts; and 3) whipping up competitive instincts.

"Two hours before . . . call the CBS affiliate and tell them the ABC affiliate is coming," he advises mischievously. "Then call the ABC outlet and tell them CBS is coming."

When organizing a debate, Verney will negotiate the date, audience composition, and (within narrow parameters) the length of statements and responses. He will also allow a campaign to veto -- not nominate – the moderator. Other alterations are not entertained.

Most Verney venues have been large halls on university campuses, loaded with students. "College facilities are relatively cheap and they often attract large capacity crowds," he explains. "If you let the station provide a studio setting, they have control. I want to maintain control of the event. So if [the TV people] balk at the expense of sending a production truck, I rent the studio and provide the security. That leaves me in control."

Verney advocates a free-form debate format staged in a living room setting of overstuffed chairs left in the open. Candidates make their opening statements, then are pitched a topic to discuss. They may ask questions and rebut answers freely, with the moderator acting as referee, awarding the floor in jump ball situations and maintaining a balance of time use. Fifteen minutes are allotted to each topic. Closings are employed, but questions from panelists or the audience are not.

"The moderator must be a well-known, trusted journalist – well-versed on the issues and able to handle the candidates," cautions the former air-traffic controller. ". . . I don't like [the use of] professional panelists. That's four unnecessary people the voter has to get to know – people they can't vote for."

Debate Sponsorship: Organizers Share Their Collective Wisdom

Surveys of those who have been political candidates find at least one point on which there is virtual unanimity: Our electoral system needs more debates with fair formats, large audiences, extensive and equitable news coverage. We also need enough debates to let candidates get their message across to the voters without expensive ad campaigns.

The public generally agrees. A 2002 survey of registered voters across the nation conducted for the Debate Advisory Standards Project (*see Chapter 5*) found 54 percent thought we have about the right amount of candidate debates. But while 35 percent thought there should be more debates, only 9 percent felt there should be fewer. And 71 percent thought debates ought to give candidates more time to explain their views on complex issues.

Why are there not enough debates, or – at least – not enough truly substantive ones? Perhaps because only one extensive, national organization – the League of Women Voters – makes debate sponsorship part of its central mission, and the League is far from omnipresent across the country. To rectify this situation, more organizations must involve themselves in the sponsorship of campaign debates, and they must do so in a manner that will assure substantive content and widespread media coverage. To achieve these goals quickly and efficiently, expert guidance is required.

To learn from the recent experiences, we surveyed debate coordinators from widely varied organizations. Between them, those interviewed have helped administer over a hundred debates. The sample was evenly divided between those groups that had concentrated on statewide campaigns, and those concerned primarily with races downballot.

Although no two debate organizers we talked to would run these events the same way, there is remarkable unanimity among these experts on a great many issues, once a context has been defined.

Below is a set of guidelines for the organization and conduction of debates, based on the responses of the veteran debate organizers we interviewed, with illustrative comments. Each point reflects a majority or median response, with a few slight adjustments to make conflicting components fit. In effect, we have utilized the surveyed coordinators as an advisory board and used their collective judgment to arrive at a recommended plan of action.

Advice on Arrangements and Formats

• How long – "Regardless of how many candidates there are, they won't stay sharp past 90 minutes," warns Russ Verney, formerly of New Hampshire Democratic Party and United We Stand. "You can't hold the audience's attention past that." If a broadcast TV station is carrying the event, it may pressure for a 55-minute format.

• TV coverage – Try to get the debate carried on radio and television – preferably a broadcast station. Offer to share the sponsorship marquee with a broadcast TV station and make their anchor the moderator, if necessary. But don't sell yourself short. "We have no trouble getting stations to partner with us on races for statewide office," reports Carol Scott of the Oklahoma LWV.

• Co-sponsors – If broadcast TV won't carry it, identify other groups that would be helpful in conducting and publicizing the debate and try to recruit them as co-sponsors. It is also "a good way to forge partnerships with other community groups that can later be useful on other fronts," notes Stacey Patricoski of the Illinois League. If you are worried about the focus of the debate wandering from your objectives, recruit only like-minded groups.

• Scheduling – Set the debate date somewhere between one and three weeks before the election, unless your primary purpose is to use it as an endorsement interview. "Most candidates will want to push them back to several weeks or even months out," warns Verney. "Organizers should try to put them in the time frame . . . when the general public is focused on the campaign: the last few weeks before the election." Be prepared to shift this date somewhat to accommodate the greatest number of candidate schedules.

• Venue – Hold the debate in a large hall, unless the only broadcast TV station that will carry it insists on using its studio. If you think you might have an overflow crowd, distribute tickets. Provide an equal number for each campaign, but reserve some for the sponsors and the general public. "Make sure you've got an accessible facility," advises the NAACP's Terry Payne, "one people know the location of, one that is easy for people to come to."

• Alerting the participants – Notify the campaigns in a low-profile race well before the event. "You want to get to them early, before their calendar starts filling up," cautions Verney. As soon as they agree or express an interest in participating, send out a formal letter of invitation, along with a copy of your debate rules and guidelines. Particularly if you are going to be carried on broadcast TV, require that a copy of the rules and guidelines be signed and returned by the candidate or campaign manager.

• Conducting negotiations – If it appears alterations to your debate setting, format or rules will be necessary to ensure the participation of one or more candidates, make each campaign in the race a party to the negotiations. Restrict negotiations to the date, physical format, stage details, and length of answers and statements. And make sure you are dealing with the boss. "We tell them to send someone who is in authority to make decisions for the campaign," declares Patricoski. "We will not leave that room until the rules are finalized." To minimize conflicts, keep candidates well-informed, well in advance. "You need to make your plans in such a way that a candidate does not feel intimidated," says Roy Miller of the Children's Campaign. "Make sure they are given adequate time to review all materials – format, rules, etc." Forming what some would call a "debate cartel" early in the campaign season is a means of avoiding negotiations altogether.

• Attracting news coverage – The closer you schedule the event to the election, the more newsworthy it will be deemed. "Send out press releases early, then start making follow-up calls to media contacts as the event moves closer," advises Greg Borum of The Citizen's Project, echoing themes offered by many. "Get a commitment from the assignment editor or news director that they will definitely send someone. Stay on them until they do. Not quite harassment, but steady follow-up." Ask the campaigns to urge their press contacts to attend. If you have a successful track record of hosting debates, dramatize it with video and newspaper clips sent out in a promotional brochure and video.

• Drawing a crowd – Make full use of free media to publicize the event. "We put [notices of the debate] in the papers, on their 'community calendar,' " recounts Payne. "We made sure notices were on community bulletin boards. Announcements were made in churches. We got it on the local cable channel for free." Choose co-sponsors, in part, according to how well they can promote the event and make sure all sponsors send various notices to their memberships. To encourage news media references to your event before it happens, make note of current campaign controversies in your press releases, suggesting a dramatic showdown in the making.

• Choosing a moderator – Select a nonpartisan moderator who is confident, knowledgeable about the issues and has a commanding stage presence. Empower them – and them only – with the ability to follow up on questions, and tightly restrict the usage. "Having flexibility for . . . follow-up is great," says Patricoski, "but we normally don't have flexibility in a tightly timed TV debate."

• Choosing panelists – Select a panel of well-informed individuals who can communicate clearly and succinctly. At least one should be a member of the news media, preferably a television reporter. "Radio people talk too much," says Scott, "and newspaper people often don't know how to talk, at least on TV." The other panelist(s) should either both be nonpartisan or each be opposing partisans.

• Screen questions from the audience – Distribute question cards through the audience, and have them screened by two members of either your organization or the League of Women Voters. Have the screeners combine similar questions and edit for length and clarity before passing them to the moderator for presentation. Never take questions directly from audience members. "Too often they spend precious time trying to make their own points," complains Scott.

• Candidate statements – Permit each candidate an opening and closing statement, but limit each statement to 2 minutes. "The opening statement serves to calm jitters," explains Verney. "The closing statement wraps up debate, summarizes positions and makes the case for your vote."

• Questioning by the panel or audience – Permit all candidates to respond to each question from the panel or audience, rotating the order in which the candidates respond. Limit these responses to reasonable lengths. Allow the moderator to ask a brief follow-up question if it is pertinent to the subject of the original question. Limit the response to half the time of the initial answer. "If a candidate's answer begs another question, it would be a shame to miss it," notes the Sierra Club's Carolyn Chase. "Or maybe they didn't answer the question." If more than two opponents are present, allow the first candidate who answers a question a short rebuttal after the others have finished. "That way he [can] respond to attacks made," explains Patricoski.

• Candidate-to-candidate questioning – Allow each candidate one or two opportunities to ask a question of another candidate. "Nobody knows better than the candidates themselves what the differences are between them," contends Patricoski. Whether the questioning candidate can rebut the answer can be left to negotiation.

• Subject matter – Do not restrict questioners to certain subjects. "It slants the debate toward the candidate who agrees with the sponsoring organization on that issue," Patricoski observes.

• Virtual debaters – Consider allowing candidates to participate in the debate by remote video hookup, if they have a compelling excuse for their absence and the process is technologically practicable. Try not to allow surrogates to substitute for a candidate. If a candidate does not show for the debate and has no compelling excuse, represent their absence with an empty chair or podium on stage. "Most of them aren't honest enough to tell you they don't want to debate," warns Chase. "They just say they have a 'scheduling conflict.' Well, find out what the scheduling conflict is and put it on the chair!"

• Reaction shots – Television crews should be permitted to use shots of candidates reacting to the comments of another candidate, but only if both candidates are seen within the frame. "Body language says as much as words do," argues Nancy Reed of the Fairfax County (Va.) Chamber of Commerce.

• Handling violators – A candidate who violates the debate rules should be cited immediately by the moderator; if the candidate persists in non-compliance he or she should be threatened with expulsion, then expelled if the behavior continues. "If you have to keep reminding them, it ruins the forum and damages your credibility," warns Borum.

• Restrictions on the audience – Members of the audience should be required to leave campaign paraphernalia outside the hall and be asked to refrain from reacting to the debate until its conclusion. "No laughing, cheering, buttons, signs or booing," orders Patricoski, echoing an often-cited litany. A significant demonstration in behalf of a certain candidate should be deducted from that candidate's time and an announcement should be made to that effect.

CHAPTER 10

Debate Participant Checklists

By Diana B. Carlin

Sponsor Checklists: Debate Planning

✔ Select a site and date and back-up date at least two months in advance. Send out a "save the date" notice to each campaign. This will enable campaigns to plan ahead or alert you to a date that won't work. The site will be dictated by whether there will be an audience, if the debate is broadcast live or taped or is broadcast at all, and accessibility for candidates and audience members.

✔ Prepare a budget (see next page).

✔ Develop a preliminary set of rules and format (including time limits, types of speeches and debate set style).

✔ Send official letters of invitation to the debate to candidates and include a copy of the rules and format. Determine if you will allow surrogates.

✔ Select a moderator and questioners (if it will be a traditional model) and a timekeeper.

✔ Organize a planning session and send letters of invitation.

✔ Send a follow-up letter to the candidates outlining final rules and format. Include all other information about the day or night of the debate such as when to arrive, where to park, availability of a preparation room for the candidate and staff, how seating will be allocated, a diagram of the stage arrangement, rules about notes and visual aids, and requests for any special needs.

✔ Publicize the debate via news releases, advertising, newsletters, etc.

✔ Print programs that include brief biographies of the candidates, names of sponsors, etc.

✔ Secure donations of goods and services.

✔ Provide participants with multiple phone numbers to get information prior to the debate. Provide phone numbers where sponsors can be reached at the debate hall the day or night of the debate. Ask campaigns to submit phone numbers for campaign staff members to be reached the day of the debate.

✔ Determine how audience seating will be arranged and prepare tickets if necessary due to limited seating.

✔ Solicit topics for questions from members of your organization or the general public. Have someone categorize the recurring question types and give the questions to the moderator and panelists.

Sponsor Checklists: Debate Budget

✔ Debate site. Is there a location that is free of charge or will you need to pay rent? Is there a set fee or is it by the hour? Remember that you will need time for setup and cleanup.

✔ Furniture. Does the site have furniture such as chairs

for the audience, lecterns, etc., available or will they have to be rented or secured from another source?

✔ Electrical. Do you need to rent microphones, sound equipment, lights, etc.? What additional power sources are necessary?

✔ Printed materials. This would include invitations, programs for audience members, publicity items and postage.

✔ Labor. Do you need to hire individuals to help set up the site and clean up afterward? Do you need to hire individuals to monitor the sound system? Do you need to hire security? Does the site supply staff that you pay on an hourly basis? If it is a televised debate, do you need a makeup artist?

✔ Transcripts/recording equipment. Do you intend to record the debate and make transcripts available?

✔ Telephone. Do you have sufficient cell phones or will you need to secure additional ones?

✔ Refreshments. Do you plan to have a reception afterward? Where possible, find someone to donate materials and services to reduce costs.

Sponsor Checklists: Debate Site

✔ Set up stage (chairs, table for moderator/panelists; lecterns, stands or tables for candidates; microphones, water, pencils and paper, timing mechanism for the timekeeper).

✔ Set up seats for audience if there are no stationary seats. Rope off sections for dignitaries or sponsors and campaign families and staff, if there is open seating. Have microphones set up in aisles for citizen questions, if they are part of the format.

✔ Set up table for materials supplied by candidates.

✔ Set up media viewing section. Be sure to have additional power sources available and tables for computers.

✔ Have stopwatches or other timing devices and time cards or signals for the timekeeper.

✔ Put programs on chairs or arrange to have ushers to distribute them as audience members arrive.

✔ Double-check all microphones. If televised or broadcast on radio, try to have a backup system.

✔ If audience questions are part of the format, have paper and pencils available for audience members to write questions. Assign ushers to collect questions if they are to be read by the moderator rather than asked directly by the audience members.

✔ Reserve parking spaces for candidates and staff. Have someone in the parking lot to greet candidates and escort them to their preparation rooms.

✔ Have candidates, moderator, panelists, etc., arrive at least one hour prior to the debate to review rules and to permit them time to test microphones, etc.

✔ Have water, soft drinks, coffee, etc., in the candidates' prep rooms.

✔ Have staff prepare refreshments for reception.

✔ Arrange for ushers to assist audience members in collecting tickets and locating seating if seating is assigned. If seating is assigned, do not give campaigns blocs of seats together. This will prevent the crowd from creating too much noise and consuming valuable debate time.

✔ Arrange interview area for post-debate interviews.

✔ Arrange for cleaning of the site and the return of borrowed or rented equipment.

✔ Have a procedure developed regarding surrogates if someone fails to attend.

Sponsor Checklists: Post-Debate Tasks

✔ Issue a news release about the debate.

✔ Send thank you letters to all participants.

✔ Distribute tapes of debates and transcripts to citizen groups, participants, and other interested individuals or groups.

✔ Contact participants and ask for suggestions for future debates.

✔ Return all borrowed or rented equipment.

✔ Send thank you letters to everyone who helped with arrangements or made donations.

✔ Prepare a file of news clippings and broadcast video or audiotapes of the debates or reports about the debates.

✔ Pay bills.

✔ Hold a staff meeting and prepare a memorandum with an analysis of the strengths and weaknesses of the event and what to do differently for the next debate.

Candidate/Campaign Checklist

✔ Review all rules and procedures for the debate. Call the sponsor if there are questions.

✔ Prepare opening and/or closing statements and practice.

✔ If general topic areas are provided, prepare brief outlines of issues for each. If topics are not available, anticipate the likely topics and prepare brief outlines of issues for each. Practice speaking on the major ideas for each issue. Try to limit your points to three per topic.

✔ Prepare questions to ask the opponent if cross-examination is included.

✔ Arrive at the debate site at least one hour early to test microphones and become familiar with the stage and the room. Find out ahead of time about the color of the backdrop to better select clothing.

✔ Bring campaign materials for display, if allowed by the rules. Some groups will allow banners.

✔ If notes are permitted, have them arranged for easy access and reference.

✔ Have a pen or pencil as a backup for what is provided by the sponsor.

✔ Be available to the media for interviews after the debate. Determine prior to the debate what issues you want discussed with the media, regardless of whether they were debated.

Moderator Checklist

✔ Review the rules and procedures.

✔ Study the key issues that may be raised during the debate as well as candidate positions on those issues.

✔ Prepare an opening statement to summarize audience and participant rules.

✔ Prepare introductions of candidates and panelists.

✔ Meet with the timekeeper to coordinate signals.

✔ Arrive at least one hour before the debate to familiarize yourself with the setting and to test microphones.

✔ Use paper and pencil to help keep track of rotation of questions.

✔ Meet with question panelists and candidates to review rules and procedures.

Questioner Checklist

✔ Review rules and procedures.

✔ Prepare questions ahead of time and coordinate with other panelists to avoid duplication.

✔ Avoid making speeches or providing lengthy introductions to questions. Consider simple structure such as, "What is your position on 'blank' issue?" Or "How do you propose to protect key state services without raising taxes?"

✔ Consult public opinion polls and the candidates' information in designing questions.

✔ Structure questions to provide comparisons of candidates' positions or to force candidates to extend their original response in follow-up or subsequent questions. Try to coordinate with other panelists to ask multiple questions on a topic rather than have a random selection of unrelated issues that allow candidates to give only sound bite responses.

✔ Arrive at least one hour before the start of the debate to coordinate with other participants and test microphones.

CHAPTER 11

Debate Watch: Getting Citizens Involved

By Diana B. Carlin

D ebate Watch is a simple idea to get voters talking about the candidates and issues, not just listening. Anyone can participate regardless of age or past political involvement.

Debate Watch began as a national project connected with the presidential debates in 1996. It was suggested by voters in the 1992 presidential election who participated in a national focus group study. The study, sponsored by The Commission on Presidential Debates, involved 625 voters in 17 cities who met after each debate to discuss what they had learned, what they still needed to know about the candidates and the issues, and what they liked and didn't like about each of the formats. Focus group members represented a cross-section of America, and the Commission on Presidential Debates (CPD) took what they had to say seriously.

The focus group members said they preferred a variety of formats, that they wanted more citizen participation through town meeting debates and that they wanted topics covered in more depth. Those suggestions shaped the 1996 and 2000 presidential debates, and those debates have influenced what happens at the state and local level.

The participants also told the CPD that they enjoyed talking about the debates and the candidates with their friends or even with people they previously did not know.

We are often told that we shouldn't discuss religion or politics in polite company. As a result, many Americans don't talk about what is happening in government and how it affects them. The result is less participation in the process. Debate Watch has proven to be a way to increase interest and voter participation.

The 1992 focus group participants found they learned as much from the discussions as they did from the debates. Many of them followed the election more closely and sought out news sources such as cable channels or the Internet for the first time. And, most importantly, they found they could disagree without becoming disagreeable. Those 625 citizens told the CPD to find a way to encourage all Americans to do what they did – watch and listen to the debates and then talk about what they had just seen and heard.

It is truly a grassroots example of democracy at work. The concept that was used in both the 1996 and 2000 presidential debates has been adapted by a variety of groups for state and local debates.

Getting Organized

Hosting or participating in a Debate Watch is easy. Make a party of it. Think of it as a political Super Bowl event. Remember, there is no single way to organize a Debate-Watch. The most important thing is to get people together to talk about the debates and about issues in the statewide, congressional, district and local races.

Below are some common questions about hosting a Debate Watch:

Q: Who can host?

A: Anyone! Or any group, formal or informal. The whole point of Debate Watch is to get as many Americans as possible talking about the debates, the campaign, the candidates and the issues that affect our lives.

Q: Who should be invited to participate?

A: Invite your neighbors, friends, co-workers or family.

Organize a Debate Watch group for members of an organization to which you belong in place of a regular meeting. Think about including people of all ages, including teens who might not be old enough to vote yet but are interested in current events. It takes no special expertise to talk about the issues so anyone you know would potentially enjoy participating.

Q: How many people should be invited?

A: Discussion works best if approximately six to 12 people participate. If you belong to a larger group or organization that wants to hold a Debate Watch, view the debate together and then break into smaller groups for post-debate discussions.

Q: Where should Debate Watch groups meet?

A: Debate Watch groups can meet in a living room, school, community center, public library, business, church or place of worship, union hall, restaurant or wherever you can watch a television and comfortably form a circle of chairs or meet around a table after the debate to discuss. Colleges and universities have had as many as 500 students and community members gather in a student union to watch and then talk. With large groups, have a large-screen television or several televisions to guarantee that everyone can see. If you are planning to divide a large gathering into multiple groups, make sure you have enough space or rooms so groups don't disturb one another. You can also meet in cyberspace. Organize a discussion with friends across the city or state who can't be in the same place the day or night of a debate.

Q: Do we need a group leader, and what qualifications should a leader have?

A: You should designate a facilitator to lead the group only to get things organized and keep discussion going. Included are suggestions for a group facilitator (See Facilitator's Guide and Sample Questions). Select someone to lead the group who is comfortable giving directions and who won't dominate the discussion. In fact, the facilitator should get others to speak and should do little speaking. If you want to hold a gathering, but no one feels comfortable leading, take turns asking questions or raising issues. You will find once you get started, you don't need a formal facilitator.

Q: Is it all right to copy this material and share it with the group?

A: Yes. Make as many copies as you need.

Q: Should we try to pick a winner?

A: No. There is no single way to select a winner. Since that is probably the least interesting and least useful question to consider, concentrate on each issue and who answered the questions better.

Q: How do we organize the evening?

A: Here is a checklist of tasks for organizing the evening, but remember you can add your own features.

✔ Duplicate "A Viewer's Guide to Political Debates," and, if possible, distribute it to participants prior to the debate.

✔ Have Debate Watch participants arrive at the viewing/discussion site about 20-30 minutes before the scheduled beginning of the debate to get acquainted and discuss the evening's events. Don't turn the television on until a few minutes before the debate begins and leave the volume off until the debate is actually ready to begin to avoid influencing discussion through exposure to candidate or media comments, in case there is news coverage before the debate starts.

✔ Arrange for seating so everyone can see the television easily. Have some soft drinks, tea, coffee and finger foods to help create a relaxed atmosphere. You might have each member of the group bring something such as ice, cups, napkins, food, etc. This should be seen as a way to build community as well as talk about the candidates.

✔ As soon as the debate ends, turn the television off. Take about 10 minutes to stretch, etc. (but try to avoid extensive informal discussion), and then have the leader gather everyone around a table or put chairs in a circle to discuss.

✔ The leader can follow the suggested set of questions, and can raise additional questions. It isn't important to ask all the questions. Talk until you run out of things to say. Most groups should be able to hold a discussion for about an hour.

✔ Some debate sponsors may be conducting research associated with formally promoted DebateWatches in a community. If they are and you want to participate, discuss the questions they are asking and reach a consensus for your responses.

✔ If you had a successful evening, make arrangements to get together again for one of the other debates, if more than one is broadcast.

Facilitator's Guide

Your role is to pose questions to the group, ensure everyone has an opportunity to speak and mediate disagreements if necessary. The attached questions are designed as suggestions only. Please feel free to revise as you see appropriate.

It is unlikely that disagreements among group members will become heated. Should this occur, diffuse the situation with a question to the individuals or a light comment.

Remind members that everyone's opinion is valuable and that everyone will have an opportunity to express an opinion. Stress that learning, rather than persuasion, is the purpose of the discussion.

Don't be afraid to politely tell someone who is dominating the discussion that his or her ideas are great, but other people may want to comment as well.

Preliminary Steps

✔ Have group members in their seats at least 5-10 minutes prior to the beginning of the debate.

✔ Do not turn the television on until a few minutes before the debate is to begin. Turn the volume on when the debate actually begins to reduce the influence of pre-debate discussions.

✔ Consider using name tags to facilitate interactions and introductions among group members. Name tags may be especially helpful if there are people who don't know one another. Group discussion will flow much easier if individuals feel comfortable speaking with other members and interacting with you. A brief period where members introduce themselves and their interests or reasons for being in the group can help break the ice.

✔ Have a pad of paper and a pen or pencil and take notes. Keep a list of the topics raised in the questions for later discussion.

Post-Debate Procedures

✔ As soon as the last speech is completed, shut the television off. Take a 10-minute break for refreshments, etc. Advise group members not to discuss the debate until they return from the break.

✔ When everyone has re-assembled, thank them for participating. Explain that this is a discussion and that there are no right or wrong answers; they are there to share their reactions to the debates and to learn from one another.

✔ Begin with the first question on the list. Ask a new question when discussion is waning. You don't have to ask all of the questions, and feel free to add questions of your own to probe someone's comments. Encourage group members to ask questions of their own.

✔ In the course of discussion, participants may answer a question that appears later, so skip it.

✔ When the discussion has waned, ask for last comments and call it an evening. It is likely that informal discussions will continue around the food and drinks.

Sample Questions

✔ What did you learn from the debate that you didn't know previously about a candidate or an issue?

✔ What do you still need to know about the candidates and the issues after the debate?

✔ Who in the group knows something from the news or other information that wasn't covered in the debate?

✔ Where can you find the information you need?

✔ What were the most important issues discussed in the debate? Are the candidates and the media doing enough to help you learn what you need to know?

✔ What is the single most important issue facing you and

your family? Did the candidates address that issue? Why do you think it wasn't raised by the candidates or the media?

✔ What do you look for in a (governor, senator, member of Congress, mayor, etc.)? How can you tell if the candidates have those qualities? What did you see and hear tonight that did or didn't convince you?

✔ There were X number of issues raised; who did better on issue 1, 2, 3, etc.?

✔ How can you influence government and officeholders?

✔ What do you expect from elected officials? From government?

✔ Was the debate more or less useful than other sources of political information?

✔ Is there anything you would change about the format?

✔ What else haven't we discussed that you want to talk about before we conclude?

A Viewer's Guide to Political Debates

Voters typically identify candidate debates as the most influential source of information received during a campaign. Because of their importance, this guide gives suggestions for getting the most out of a debate.

Structure of Debates

Debates use a variety of formats. Primary debates (featuring candidates from the same party) and local debates traditionally are more freewheeling, and incorporate a wide range of formats because of multiple candidates. Since 1992, the general election presidential debates also have featured multiple set styles, including a town meeting with citizen questioners.

Most debates impose time limits on answers to ensure all candidates have equal opportunity to respond. Topics may focus on a wide range of issues or concentrate on a particular theme, such as education or the economy. General election presidential debates usually divide the time between foreign and domestic topics.

Candidates may have an opening statement, or a moderator may introduce each candidate and begin questioning immediately. In most debates, candidates have closing statements. In some debates, candidates have both opening and closing statements.

Questions guide the content of debates. There are three types of questions: initial, follow-up and cross-examination. Initial questions get the debate started by asking candidates to explain or defend a position, or compare it with an opponent's. Many initial questions are hypotheticals in the form of, "What would you do if ...?"

Follow-up questions are directed at a candidate after an answer is given. Their purpose is to probe the original response by asking for elaboration or clarification. Some may focus on an unrelated topic. Follow-up questions may be asked immediately after an initial response is given or after all candidates have answered the initial question.

Cross-examination questions are questions that one candidate addresses to another. A separate time can be set aside for cross-examination questions or they may be included as follow-ups.

Questions may be posed to candidates from a variety of sources. In primary and local debates, experts on the topic debated may serve as panelists. A single moderator (usually from the media) or a panel of media representatives or subject experts are the most common questioners.

Many debates, especially at the local level, allow for questions from the audience at some point in the debate. The Richmond, Va., town meeting in 1992 was the first general election presidential debate to involve citizen questioners. Recent innovations include questions from remote sources or questions sent to a moderator via the Internet.

Getting the Most Out of Debates

Focus your attention on a few key points. Know what it is you want in an officeholder, then watch and listen to see which candidate best fits your ideal. The following suggestions will help you focus:

✔ Prepare ahead. Try to follow the campaign at least a few weeks before the first debate.

✔ Watch more than one debate. No debate can cover every issue; try to watch multiple debates to learn the most.

✔ Watch with others. Once the debate is over, discuss what you heard and saw. Research shows that discussion helps clarify points made in the debate.

✔ Set aside your partisan views. Use the debates to learn as much as possible about all candidates and their positions.

✔ Don't worry about who won or lost. All the sides will claim victory. Since there are no criteria for determining a political debate winner, concentrate more on issues and ideas rather than on strategies. Focus on the question, "Who would make a better president, senator, governor, legislator, county clerk?"

✔ Pay close attention to the candidates when they talk about how to solve problems. Listen carefully for comparisons candidates make between or among their programs and those of their opponents.

✔ Identify the candidate's debate goals. Does the candidate speak directly to the issues, provide specifics, and present new policies or information? Or does the candidate evasively interpret questions to suit his/her agenda?

✔ Identify the images candidates try to create for themselves. Most candidates try to portray themselves as leaders and identify themselves with cherished American values, while suggesting their opponents lack these qualities. What in the responses supports their claims?

✔ Be aware of the limitations of televised debates. Television works by showing action. To create action and minimize monotony, directors sometimes include "reaction shots" to show one candidate's response to an opponent's statement. This can distract your attention from what is being said. It is wise to remember the role of action shots when watching the debates.

✔ Try to learn more after the debate. Because most formats provide for brief responses, it is difficult to get a complete understanding of a candidate's position or the issues discussed. Follow up on the issues by watching and reading the news or visiting candidates' Web sites.

About the Guide: *This guide was adapted from material by the following National Communication Association members: Diana B. Carlin, University of Kansas; Robert Friedenberg, Miami University, Hamilton, Ohio; James Guadino, National Communication Association; Susan Hellweg, San Diego State University; John Morello, Mary Washington College; Michael Pfau, University of Oklahoma.*

CHAPTER 12

Debate Literature: Previous Research Findings

By Peter L. Francia

Impact of Debates on Voter Knowledge and Behavior

Citizens watch debates for a variety of reasons. The most common explanation viewers mention is learning about candidates' positions on issues. Other considerations for viewing a debate include the desire to remain informed about politics or civic obligation (Sears and Chaffee 1979, 228).

Debates provide the electorate with an extensive and sustained view of the candidates' personalities and positions on the issues (Kraus 2000, 6; Jamieson and Birdsell 1988, 126) and expose partisans to opposing views, which may make it easier for the electorate to accept election results (Lubell 1962, 152). Debates also allow the electorate to compare differences between the candidates and to see how candidates respond to questions and challenges under pressure. Jamieson and Birdsell (1988, 131-132) explain:

In debates candidates answer questions viewed as central by their opponents in an environment in which the electorate can compare the answers. Where in stump speeches candidates tend to indict their opponents, in debate the threat of imminent rebuttal invites a response to charges pending against one's candidacy. In debates one engages both in case-building and refutation. Consequently debates are able, though they do not always do this, to produce a clarity and specificity otherwise absent in campaign discourse.

Debates are important because they can generate public interest in campaigns, especially in close elections (Denton and Woodward 1990, 102). They can also change citizens' notions of a candidate's viability. Debates held during the 1996 Arizona Republican presidential primary, for example, influenced respondents' assessments of the candidates' electability and in some instances changed voter preferences (Yawn, Ellsworth, Beatty, and Kahn 1998). When candidates were able to break citizens' expectations in a positive manner, they were more likely to attract additional support. Conversely, when candidates disappointed followers in a debate, they often lost support.

The effect of debates on voter preferences is a function of citizens' political knowledge and the strength of their beliefs. Debates influence candidate preferences most among the least politically attentive voters (Miller and MacKuen 1979, 277), those with low levels of political knowledge (Abramowitz 1978, 182) and those weakly committed to a particular candidate (Sears, Freedman, and O'Connor 1964; Geer 1988, 494). Sears and Chaffee (1979, 247) explain:

It is an obvious point, but important to document, that weak initial attitudes changed most. This is clearest in immediate post-debate image changes. After the first debate there was much greater change among those with no (or wavering) predebate vote choices.

The number of debates that citizens view can further affect which candidates voters will support. Typically, those interested in politics are more likely to watch and receive information about debates than those who are not (Sears and Chaffee 1979, 233). However, sporadic debate viewers are the ones most influenced by debates (Abramowitz 1978, 175). Voters who did not view debates rarely switched their preferences to a different candidate (Chaffee 1978, 342).

Debates, in addition to sometimes informing vote choice, more often serve as a reinforcement of prior beliefs. Sears and Chaffee (1979, 244) explain, "[I]nformation flowing from the debates appears to have promoted higher levels of consistency among voters' party identifications, candidate evaluations, issue positions, and vote intentions." Partisan voters who think the candidate of their party won the debate "come home" after debates because "they are reminded why they are Democrats or Republicans" (Geer 1988, 493). Partisan voters also can become more committed to a candidate after viewing debates in which the opposition presents information contradictory to their beliefs (Sears, Freedman, and O'Connor 1964).

In addition to partisanship, the ideological leanings of the voters may influence their assessment of a debate. Sigelman and Sigelman (1984), for example, found that the ideological beliefs of undecided voters influenced their views on whether Carter or Reagan won the 1980 presidential debate. They (1984, 627) write:

It is clear that the public does not approach presidential debates cognitively unencumbered and determined to weigh the evidence evenhandedly. Only when the powerful impacts of prior beliefs and preferences are considered can one fully understand why presidential debates have not had the marked influence on election outcomes that many early observers anticipated.

Still, some research suggests that debates do not reinforce citizens' pre-existing biases. An analysis of the 1988 presidential debates, for example, found that respondents remained unsure about which candidate they preferred after viewing the second Bush-Dukakis debate. The debate also did not increase issue agreement between candidates and their supporters (Lanoue 1991, 91). Others conclude that the overall effects of debates on the electorate are minimal (Sears and Chaffee 1979, 244).

Nevertheless, debates can serve as an important source of political information. Debates are often helpful in heightening voter knowledge of lesser-known candidates (Zhu, Milavsky, and Biswas 1994; Holbrook 1999, 79). Undecided voters, in particular, often look to the debates for information about the candidates' policy positions and learn from them (Lang and Lang 1961, 282; Chaffee 1978; Pfau 1988; Holbrook 1999, 84). An analysis of the 1976 Ford-Carter debate, for example, showed an increase in voters' awareness of political issues (Chaffee 1978) and of the candidates' positions (Abramowitz 1978, 683-684). Those who watched the second Bush-Dukakis debate also retained information on the candidates' positions, although the effects of information gains diminished over two weeks (Lanoue 1991). Debates are even effective among non-viewers.

Citizens who do not watch debates still experience a gain in issue awareness, primarily through exposure to media reports about the debate or from conversations with friends and family (Abramowitz 1978, 684). Learning and information acquisition tends to occur predominantly from early debates. Holbrook (1999, 77) writes:

Early debates represent the best opportunity for voters to acquire information about the candidates. This may indicate that by the time the second and third debates roll around later in the campaign, voters have less use for the information, either because they have heard it all before (perhaps in the first debate) or they have decided how to vote and are closed off to new information.

Additionally, viewers may view topics covered in the debate as more important than they would have before the debate. One study of the 1976 Carter-Ford presidential debate reported:

Prior to the debate, these subjects ranked economic and foreign policy issues consistently high, as did the agenda of the news media they followed. The focus of the debate, however, was entirely on domestic issues .... Following the debate, these [domestic] issues remained high on viewers' personal agendas while foreign policy and defense issues (which had not been dis-

cussed in the debate) decreased in importance (Swanson and Swanson 1978, 352).

Indeed, the candidate's ability to shape the issue agenda is a significant matter. The candidates' issue positions often outweigh other factors in influencing voter preferences. Dyson and Scioli (1974, 85-86) report that vote choice was "generally dependent on specific issue positions of the candidates rather than highly general factors derived from their personal appeal." The authors add, "mentioning specific issues relevant to the campaign situation is perceived by respondents as the really dominant factor in arriving at vote choices."

On the other hand, debates may instruct the electorate more on the debaters' personality than on issues (Becker, Weaver, Graber, and McCombs 1979). Others are critical of debates because they are not always a strong forum to communicate solutions to complicated issues. Zhu, Milavsky, and Biswas (1994, 305-206) explain:

Discourse on policy issues requires both problem description and solution prescription. ... Candidates in televised debates can portray the symptoms of social problems quite graphically, usually as an effective means to attack an opponent. When it comes to solutions to the problems, the participating candidates at best offer slogans, assertions, and other condensed statements suitable for sound bites.

Political debates, therefore, have some drawbacks as vehicles for candidates to detail specific solutions to problems. However, debates can have an impact on citizens' perceptions of a candidate's viability and can serve to reinforce a voter's political predispositions. More significantly, debates appear to inform some voters about political issues and to influence their vote choices.

Media Coverage of Debates

Media coverage of debates is important in several respects. First, debates are more newsworthy than other forms of political communication and have a tendency to draw larger amounts of viewers by non-entertainment television standards (Kendall 1997; Benoit, McKinney, and Holbert 2001, 259-260). This includes presidential primary debates.

The Al Gore-Bill Bradley 2000 debate on NBC's *Meet the Press* had an audience of 4.73 million (Schroeder 2000, 109). Debates provide a story for the press to cover with the election, in many instances, still months away. CNN's Tom Hannon remarked, "For news organizations it's important to be the place people think of when they want to learn more about any kind of news. And political campaign news is a big prestige item" (quoted in Schroeder 2000, 109).

Second, media coverage is significant in boosting the ratings of little-known candidates, broadening issue coverage and perceptions of candidates' images (Davis 1999, 346). Third, voters are more likely to retain themes stressed by the media in post-debate coverage. Miller and MacKuen (1979, 281) concluded that the "aspects of the debates that viewers remembered most readily – candidate performance, competence and personality – were quite prevalent in the media coverage of the debates."

However, the "spin" or "bias" in news reporting of debates appears to have little effect on citizens' assessments of the debate. Lowry, Bridges, and Barefield (1990) studied the first Bush-Dukakis debate in 1988 and concluded that post-debate commentary served primarily to reinforce voters' predispositions. On the other hand, the authors find evidence that instant nationwide surveys conducted by the news networks may have some influence on voters' assessments of the candidate's performance. They (1990, 824) report:

Perhaps the most interesting finding to come out of this study is the apparent effect of ABC's nationwide voter survey which indicated that Dukakis had won the debate. ABC was the only network that presented survey results of this type, and ABC viewers in this study were the only group of which a majority said that Dukakis had won the debate.

Sears and Chaffee (1979, 239) came to a similar conclusion based on their analysis of the 1976 presidential debate. They write:

Rather, the news media quickly established a consensual answer to the question of which candidate had won a debate, partly through immediate reporting of poll results. This in turn guided public responses to that question, as if it were the 'correct' answer, and eventually it became so.

Some scholars are critical of the media for the emphasis they place on reporting a "winner" and a "loser." This type of reporting encourages candidates to "score against one another rather than actually debate" (Hellweg and Phillips 1981, 68). It also can have the negative effect of reducing debates to "horse races" rather than forums that help voters make informed decisions (Kraus 2000, 165-168).

Other problems with "horse race" reporting of debates concern how the media determine a "winner." Typically, the media select a winner based on which candidates avoided the fewest errors, miscalculations and contradictions rather than which candidate offered the most thoughtful and original solutions to complicated problems (Polsby 1976, 177-178). Others conclude that to win a debate a candidate does not have to put on an incredible performance, but merely surpass expectations (Yawn, Ellsworth, Beatty, and Kahn 1998).

Other studies have focused on network coverage of audience reaction shots. The primary finding is that audience reactions shots do not alter the opinions of viewers on controversial issues. They can change the persuasiveness of an argument, but not perception of the speaker's overall credibility. Davis (1999, 488) writes:

No evidence was found to support the hypothesis that reaction shots directly affect overall attitudes towards a position on an issue, or that they influence ratings of a speaker's credibility. Minimal evidence was found to suggest the reaction shots may influence ratings of the persuasiveness of a particular argument made by a speaker.

Impact of Debates on Campaign Strategies

Debates occur when certain conditions are present. Typically debates take place when: (1) the election is close; (2) both candidates expect to gain some advantage; (3) both candidates are confident in their debating skills; (4) there are at least two major candidates; and (5) the debate format offers minimal risk for potential gaffes (Friedenberg 1979). Debates can offer several advantages to candidates.

First, an impressive debate performance can spur a campaign's fundraising efforts (Jamieson and Birdsell 1988, 157). Second, candidates who are behind in the polls can gain exposure and may potentially stall their opponent's rise (Martel 1983, 139-140).

Candidates in the lead often benefit from debates by using them as a mechanism to expand their base of support and to reinforce the preferences of their supporters (Martel 1983, 33).

Despite the popular belief that challengers have the most to gain from debates, incumbents are often the primary beneficiaries. Martel (1983, 33) explains, "The leading candidate, then, unless he is clearly outperformed, normally will reinforce the preferences of more supporters than will his opponent perhaps turn some of his 'soft' supporters into 'hard' supporters."

However, candidates must perform well to benefit from a debate. This requires a number of strategic considerations. Incumbents tend to follow "sell-oriented" strategies, often stressing their safe record of constituent service rather than employing a more controversial issues-oriented approach. Challengers, on the other hand, are more likely to engage in attack strategies that focus on controversial policy issues that could alienate the incumbent from certain voters. (Attack strategies are also more common at lower levels of office because major "breakthroughs" are often necessary for the large percentage of candidates who face obstacles in party registration, incumbency status or a combination of the two). In open-seat elections, the candidate of the "out" party often attempts to associate his opponent with any problems that could be linked to the incumbent administration, while the candidate "under attack either dissociates himself from or defends it" (Martel 1983, 63-72).

In addition, campaign advisers often instruct candidates to avoid specific answers to questions because they have little to gain by offering detailed responses (Jamieson and Birdsell 1988, 167). Avoiding specificity is a crucial element to avoiding attack. Martel (1983, 102) notes:

There are three major reasons for a candidate to avoid specificity ... (1) He may not know much about the issue in question; (2) specific commitments may be politically dangerous ... (3) a specific approach to one issue may consume time that might better be spent on another issue.

Candidates can overcome the charge that they lack sufficient political knowledge by making effective use of statistics and factual information in a debate (Martel 1983, 106). However, candidates must be careful in their use of visual aids, which can draw attention to specific points, but bear the risk of appearing "staged." Martel (1983, 107) writes:

The use of objects is not without risk. For this reason, advisers to frontrunners sometimes attempt during format negotiations to prevent them. A notable example of such a tactic backfired during a 1978 Pennsylvania Congressional race debate between Robert Edgar and Eugene "Sonny" Kane, when Kane, emphasizing the purchase of American products, held up a picture of Edgar's Volvo. As many audience members were reacting to this tactic as a gimmicky cheap shot and to an extent, as an unwar-

ranted invasion of Edgar's privacy, Edgar cleverly retorted by offering anyone in the audience a ride home in his new Plymouth.

Finally, campaigns must make strategic decisions concerning including minor party candidates in the debates. In some instances, the inclusion of minor party candidates can have some advantages for major party candidates. First, including minor party candidates often diminishes the "winner/loser" dichotomy of a two-person debate, which can assist the frontrunner. Second, debates that include minor party candidates must either reduce the number of questions or the time allotted for answers. This format may be helpful to candidates who have difficulty developing lengthy responses (Martel 1983, 51-52).

Debate Formats

Debates have come under fire for several reasons: their lack of focus, dependency on panels and the lack of true "debate" between candidates (Auer 1962; Bitzer and Reuter 1980). Many debate experts have been critical of the failure of debate rules and formats to address these shortcomings. Carlin (1994, 11) summarized six weaknesses with debates outlined in past research:

(1) There is inadequate time for substantive responses by the candidates; (2) candidates do not always answer the same question, thus reducing opportunity for comparison; (3) the question-answer format is not a debate format; (4) panelists play an overly intrusive role; (5) panelists do not reflect the public interest; (6) candidates do not answer the questions and formats do not force them to.

Yet, more recent research disputes some of these criticisms, reporting instead that political debates often involve sufficient confrontation, comparison, extension and analysis (or "clash") between candidates (Carlin, Howard, Stanfield, and Reynolds 1991; Benoit and Wells 1996).

Clash is often most pronounced under certain formats, such as traditional panel or single moderator debates with the candidates standing behind a lectern (Carlin, Howard, Stanfield, and Reynolds 1991; Carlin, Morris, and Smith 2001). Conversational debates with candidates seated at a table, on the other hand, are often less adversarial, and are often characterized by their emphasis on voter education (Carlin, Morris, and Smith 2001). Town meeting debates also tend to reduce the frequency of personal attacks (Benoit and Wells 1996).

The power of the moderator is another important aspect of debate formats and rules that can influence the tone of a debate. Carlin, Morris, and Smith (2001, 2210) found that the moderator, Jim Lehrer, directed George W. Bush and Al Gore toward clash strategies in the 2000 presidential debates. The scope of the moderator's authority is important because the position commands responsibilities that can include introducing the candidates, acting as a possible questioner or even coaxing legitimate answers from non-responsive candidates.

With respect to the latter power, most candidates prefer rules that do not allow the moderator to have the authority to interrupt them (Martel 1983, 143-144). Some campaigns agree to debates that permit audience questioning. In these instances, the debate should rely on pre-screened questions. Questions that are not pre-screened "pose the risk that the person selected may issue a statement instead of a question, debate one or more of the candidates, be unduly biased, engage in a struggle for control with the moderator, or pursue an irrelevant or overly repetitious line of questioning" (Martel 1983, 144).

In addition to audience questioning, campaigns must also decide whether to allow the candidates to directly question one another. Direct examination can have several important consequences. First, the candidate "must assess the extent to which his opponent might 'turn the tables' on him. Second, the direct give and take, as implied above, is conducive to escalating emotions with all its attendant risks. [Third]...the direct question ... can give more equal stature to both candidates" (Martel 1983, 86).

A few scholars are also critical of panel debates on the grounds that journalists provide a buffer between the competing candidates. This changes the nature of the adversarial relationship from politician-politician to questioner-politician (Jamieson and Birdsell 1988, 195). Journalists may pose questions that are too detailed and specific for the public to comprehend. Jamieson and Birdsell (1988, 169-173) write:

[Reporters] are more knowledgeable about the candidates' stands than most of the electorate. Questions designed to elicit news do not invite the level of basic information on candidate positions and differences that the less educated viewer would find useful. ... Not only are reporters' questions occasionally unnecessarily technical, but when contradictory accounts of events, acts, and discourse are offered, nothing in the existing format provides a neutral voice able to tell the confused viewer which, if either, is accurate.

Some contend that the counterrebuttal removes some of the weaknesses of the panel by allowing for more direct conflict and debate among the candidates. Martel (1983, 136-137) explains:

The counterrebuttal ... allows the candidate who initially answers a question to speak again after his opponent's rebuttal. It, therefore, provides for more clash between the candidates. Moreover, it can serve as a viable substitute for risk-prone follow-up questions for the candidate who tends to be general or the one who is not sufficiently informed.

Another criticism of political debates is that they do not provide adequate time for candidates to provide sufficient answers to complicated issues. This reinforces "sound bite politics," which many political observers lament. Jamieson and Birdsell (1988, 196) explain:

*Debate values an advocate's ability to distill complex materi-
al into manageable blocks of time. Such a facility is valuable
until the time pressures become so intense that slogans displace
argument. In televised debates, candidates are asked to perform
miracles of compression, explaining complex positions on major
issues in less than a minute.*

However, suggestions to lengthen the time for answers
have some drawbacks. First, modern audiences may not have
the attention spans to listen to time-consuming answer formats (Jamieson and Birdsell 1988, 196). Second, few candidates use all the time allotted under current restrictions
(Martel 1983, 137-138). Third, candidates might be unwilling to accept debate invitations under extended time formats. Martel (1983, 125-126) writes:

*Nor is the opportunity to present extended discussions of poli-
cy likely to appeal to candidates who lack the necessary speaking
skills, are less informed than their opponent, or have fewer
resources to research and develop issue positions. In short, the
typical panel formats are probably more congruent with the
goals, strategies, and resources of most candidates.*

Debates with a stated proposition or issue are one possible
remedy to improve the quality of discourse. However, campaigns typically shun proposition-centered debates despite
the fact that they are considered the standard for traditional
forensic debates. Martel (1983, 120) writes:

*In political debates, a defined proposition is commonly regard-
ed as restrictive and risk-prone. Candidates may be wary of plac-
ing too much weight on one specific issue, unable to disagree about
a proposition of sufficient importance to the electorate to merit
attention, fearful that a proposition will favor the opponent –
particularly if he is an incumbent more familiar with the issue
and with greater research facilities at his disposal – or concerned
that such a focus might favor the better debater.*

The challenge for structuring debate formats is thus to create an environment that allows candidates enough time to answer questions beyond the sound bite without unduly boring the audience or discouraging the candidates from participating.

The author thanks David Clifford for research assistance and Paul Herrnson, director of the Center for American Politics and Citizenship at the University of Maryland, for helpful comments and suggestions throughout this project.

Bibliography

Abramowitz, Alan I. 1978. "The Impact of a Presidential Debate on Voter Rationality." *American Journal of Political Science* 22: 680–690.

Auer, Jeffrey J. 1962. "The Counterfeit Debates." In *The Great Debates*, ed. Sidney Kraus. Bloomington, Ind.: Indiana University Press.

Benoit, William L., and William T. Wells. 1996. *Candidates in Conflict: Persuasive Attack and Defense in the 1992 Presidential Debates.* Tuscaloosa, Ala.: University of Alabama Press.

Benoit, William L., Mitchell S. McKinney, and R. Lance Holbert. 2001. "Beyond Learning and Persona: Extending the Scope of Presidential Debate Effects." *Communication Monographs* 68: 259–273.

Bitzer, Lloyd, and Theodore Reuter. 1980. *Carter v. Ford: The Counterfeit Debates of 1976.* Madison, Wis.: University of Wisconsin Press.

Carlin, Diana B. 1994. "A Rationale for a Focus Group Study." In *The 1992 Presidential Debates in Focus*, ed. Diana B. Carlin and Mitchell S. McKinney. Westport, Conn.: Praeger.

Carlin, Diana B., Eric Morris, Shawna Smith. 2001. "The Influence of Format and Questions on Candidates' Strategic Argument Choices in the 2000 Presidential Debates." *American Behavioral Scientist* 44: 2196-2218.

Carlin, Diana B., C. Howard, S. Stanfield, L. Reynolds. 1991. "The Effects of Presidential Debate Formats on Clash: A Comparative Analysis." *Argumentation and Advocacy* 27: 126-136.

Chaffee, Steven H. 1978. "Presidential Debates - Are they helpful to voters?" *Communication Monographs* 45: 330-346.

Davis, Stacy. 1999. "The Effects of Audience Reaction Shots on Attitudes Towards Controversial Issues." *Journal of Broadcasting and Electronic Media* 43: 476-491.

Denton, Robert E., and Gary Woodward. 1990. *Political Communication in America*. New York: Praeger.

Dyson, James W. and Frank P. Scioli, Jr. 1974. "Communication and Candidate Selection: Relationships of Information and Personal Characteristics to Vote Choice." *Social Science Quarterly* 55: 77-90.

Friedenberg, Robert V. 1979. " 'We are present here today for the purpose of having a joint discussion': The Conditions Requisite for Political Debates." *Journal of the American Forensic Association* 16: 1-9.

Geer, John G. 1988. "The Effects of Presidential Debates on the Electorate's Preferences for Candidates." *American Politics Quarterly* 16: 486-501.

Hellweg, Susan and Steven L. Phillips. 1981. "Form and Substance: A Comparative Analysis of Five Formats Used in the 1980 Presidential Debates." *Speaker and Gavel* 18: 67-76.

Holbrook, Thomas M. 1999. "Political Learning from Presidential Debates." *Political Behavior* 21: 67- 89.

Jamieson, Kathleen Hall, and David S. Birdsell. 1988. *Presidential Debates*. New York: Oxford University Press.

Katz, Elihu, and Jacob J. Feldman. 1962. "The Debate in the Light of Research: A Survey of Surveys." In *The Great Debates*, ed. Sidney Kraus. Bloomington, Ind.: Indiana University Press.

Kendall, Kathleen E. 1997. "Presidential Debates Through Media Eyes." *American Behavioral Scientist* 40: 1193-1207.

Kraus, Sidney. 2000. *Televised Presidential Debates and Public Policy*. Mahwah, N.J.: Lawrence Erlbaum Associates.

Lang, Kurt, and Gladys Engel Lang. 1961. "Ordeal by Debate: Viewer Reactions." *Public Opinion Quarterly* 25: 277-288.

_____. 1962. "Reactions of Viewers." In *The Great Debates*, ed. Sidney Kraus. Bloomington, Ind.: Indiana University Press.

Lanoue, David J. 1991. "The 'Turning Point': Viewers' Reactions to the Second 1988 Presidential Debate." *American Politics Quarterly* 19: 80–95.

_____. 1992. "One That Made a Difference: Cognitive Consistency, Political Knowledge, and the 1980 Presidential Debate." *Public Opinion Quarterly* 56: 168-184.

Lowry, Dennis T., Janet A. Bridges, and Paul A. Barefield. 1990. "Effects of TV 'Instant Analysis and Querulous Criticism': Following the First Bush-Dukakis Debate." *Journalism Quarterly* 67: 814–825.

Lubell, Samuel. 1962. *"Personalities vs. Issues."* In *The Great Debates*, ed. Sidney Kraus. Bloomington, Ind.: Indiana University Press.

Martel, Myles. 1983. *Political Campaign Debates*. New York: Longman.

Matera, Frances R. and Michael B. Salwen. 1996. *"Unwieldy Questions? Circuitous Answers? Journalists as Panelists in Presidential Election Debates."* Journal of Broadcasting & Electronic Media 40: 309-317.

Milic, Louis T. 1979. *"Grilling the Pols: Q&A at the Debates."* In *The Great Debates*, ed. Sidney Kraus. Bloomington, Ind.: Indiana University Press.

Miller, Arthur H. and Michael MacKuen. 1979. *"Informing the Electorate: A National Study."* In *The Great Debates*, ed. Sidney Kraus. Bloomington, Ind.: Indiana University Press.

Pfau, Michael. 1988. *"Intraparty Political Debates and Social Learning."* Journal of Applied Communication Research 16: 99-112.

Polsby, Nelson. 1976. *"Debatable Thoughts on Debates."* In *The Past and Future of Presidential Debates*, ed. Austin Ramsey. Washington, D.C.: American Enterprise Institute for Public Policy Research.

Salant, Richard S. 1979. *"The Good But Not Great Nondebates: Some Random Personal Notes."* In *The Great Debates*, ed. Sidney Kraus. Bloomington, Ind.: Indiana University Press.

Schroeder, Alan. 2000. *"Media Sponsorship of the 2000 Presidential Debates."* Press/Politics 5: 104-111.

Sears, David O. and Steven H. Chaffee. 1979. "Uses and Effects of the 1976 Debates: An Overview of Empirical Studies." In The Great Debates, ed. Sidney Kraus. Bloomington, Ind.: Indiana University Press.

Sears, David O., Jonathan L. Freedman, and Edward F. O'Connor, Jr. 1964. "The Effects of Anticipated Debate and Commitment on the Polarization of Audience Opinion." Public Opinion Quarterly 28:615-627

Siepmann, Charles A. 1962. "Were They 'Great'? " In The Great Debates, ed. Sidney Kraus. Bloomington, Ind.: Indiana University Press.

Sigelman, Lee and Carol K. Sigelman. 1984. "Judgements of the Carter-Reagan Debate: The Eyes of the Beholders." Public Opinion Quarterly 48: 624-628.

Swanson, Linda L., and David L. Swanson. 1978. "The Agenda-Setting Function of the First Ford-Carter Debate." Communication Monographs 45: 347-353.

Tiemens, Robert K. 1978. "Television's Portrayal of the 1976 Presidential Debates: An Analysis of Visual Content." Communication Monographs 45: 362- 370.

Tyler, Gus. 1984. "Democracy vs. Mediacracy." The New Leader (May 28): 10-12.

Weiss, Robert O. 1981. "The Presidential Debates in their Political Context: The Issue-Image Interface in the 1980 Campaign." Speaker and Gavel 18: 22-33.

Yawn, Mike, Kevin Ellsworth, Bob Beatty, and Kim Fridkin Kahn. 1998. "How a Presidential Primary Debate Changed Attitudes of Audience Members." Political Behavior 20: 155-181.

Zhu, Jian-Hua, J. Ronald Milavsky, and Rahul Biswas. 1994. "Do Televised Debates Affect Image Perception More than Issue Knowledge? A Study of the First 1992 Presidential Debates." Human Communication Research 20: 302–333.